Horst Schmidt-Brümmer
Paul v. Naredi-Rainer

3 x Days COLOGNE

CITY GUIDE

VISTA POINT VERLAG

Contents

I	**3 x Cologne – Key to the Cathedral City**	6
II	**Colonia – Köln – Cologne** Chronological History of the City *by Gerta Wolff*	8
III	**»Economic Center-West«** or: How Cologne Makes a Living *by Gerhard Knauf* .	17
IV	**Two Art Quarters at Your Service!** The Art Scene in Cologne *by Christiane Vielhaber* .	22
V	**Hotels in Cologne**	26
VI	**THE METROPOLIS ON THE RHINE**	
Day 1	**Between the Cathedral and the River:** The Heart of Cologne . . . Cathedral – Wallraf-Richartz-Museum/Ludwig Museum – Hohenzollernbrücke – Messeturm – Deutzer Brücke – Old Town – Gross St. Martin – Rheingarten – Cathedral	28
Day 2	**From Roman Roots to Post-Modern Times:** The Inner City of Cologne . Römisch-Germanisches Museum – Praetorium – Rathaus – Gürzenich – St. Maria im Kapitol – Schildergasse – Olivandenhof – Neumarkt – St. Aposteln – Mittelstrasse – Pfeilstrasse – Friesenviertel – St. Gereon – Römerturm – Stadtmuseum – St. Andreas	57

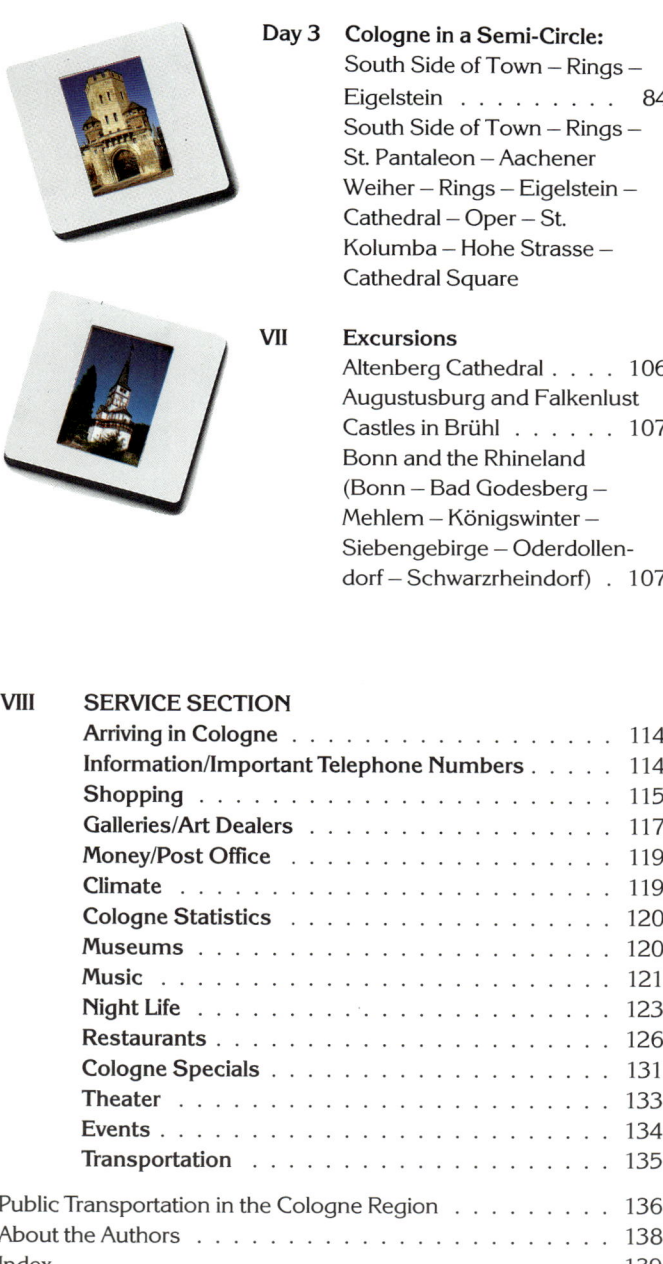

Day 3	**Cologne in a Semi-Circle:**
	South Side of Town – Rings – Eigelstein 84
	South Side of Town – Rings – St. Pantaleon – Aachener Weiher – Rings – Eigelstein – Cathedral – Oper – St. Kolumba – Hohe Strasse – Cathedral Square

VII	**Excursions**
	Altenberg Cathedral 106
	Augustusburg and Falkenlust Castles in Brühl 107
	Bonn and the Rhineland (Bonn – Bad Godesberg – Mehlem – Königswinter – Siebengebirge – Oderdollendorf – Schwarzrheindorf) . 107

VIII SERVICE SECTION

Arriving in Cologne	114
Information/Important Telephone Numbers	114
Shopping	115
Galleries/Art Dealers	117
Money/Post Office	119
Climate	119
Cologne Statistics	120
Museums	120
Music	121
Night Life	123
Restaurants	126
Cologne Specials	131
Theater	133
Events	134
Transportation	135
Public Transportation in the Cologne Region	136
About the Authors	138
Index	139
Photo Credits	141

3 × Cologne – Key to the Cathedral City

»Cities, like people, can be recognized by their pace«, Robert Musil once wrote. Cologne, the metropolis on the Rhine, is no exception. It, too, has its own pace, its unique characteristics, both functional as well as commonplace.

This city guide will focus upon them during the course of three well-proven daily routes, which will bring together much of which is specifically Cologne: science and other sightworthy places, as well as the luxurious and the stimulating. Each day, each schedule of points of interest, offers in content and timing, diversified frames of orientation – for historical and cultural highlights, as well as for insignificant trivia. In short, this small volume presents a reliable insight into Cologne to visitors who may have little time, but do have much curiosity. It is therefore neither geared to rigid sightseeing, nor is it an art lexicon with universal claim to eternity.

In order to clarify and supplement the handy short programs, the most important information about places along the routes is always summarized on the blue pages preceding the narratives. At one glance, addresses, hours and telephone numbers can be spotted.

The first day in the cathedral city one explores the Cologne nucleus with its triad of cathedral, river, and great art in the new buildings of the Wallraf-Richartz-Museum and the Ludwig Museum. It is an excursion of perspectives and pauses – of walking and looking, resting and observing.

The tour of the second day brings to life further aspects of the city center with its places of Roman culture, Romanesque church-

es, medieval secular building and modern business centers – an easy way to stroll through two thousand years of city history.

The third day once again expands the city's horizon, leading through the urbane life of a Cologne »*Veedel*« into the southern part of the city, across the recently recreated rings, back into the new center around WDR.

Some suggestions for excursions into the surroundings of Cologne, and a service section with helpful Cologne dates, as well as recommendations for restaurants, bars and discos, round out the city guide. However, in order to get a real taste of Cologne, in addition to side trips into the great art, one or more leaps into the effervescing pleasure spots should not be missed. In general, only those of Cologne's numerous stores which are situated along the routes, are mentioned.

Naturally, the pre-arranged daily schedules are only suggestions. There is nothing against departing here and there from the prescribed routes to make discoveries on one's own initiative. These tours open Cologne to both the new visitor who is still green behind the ears as well as to visitors looking for something off the beaten track. The same freedom of choice applies also to any chosen sequence of days that proceed from Cologne's inner core outward to its suburbs.

Whether in whole or in part, the routes are in any case invitations – to art, to enjoyment and to an urban experience which takes time but also allows you time. Three times.

View of Cologne's Panorama from Deutz

II Colonia — Köln — Cologne
Chronological History of the City

by Gerta Wolff

38 or 19 B. C. General Agrippa, friend and son-in-law of Emperor Augustus, governor of Gaul, establishes a settlement for the Germanic Ubier tribe, which he transfers from the right to the left side of the Rhine. The center of the OPPIDUM UBIORUM was a widely known imperial shrine, the ARA UBIORUM.

50 A. D. Agrippina, born in the Ubier settlement in 15 A. D., granddaughter of Agrippa, and wife of Emperor Claudius, acquired for Cologne the right to create its own by-laws, as well as a new name. This name embraces a brief history of its foundation: C(olonia) C(laudia) A(ra) A(grippinensium), »the city which was established under Claudius on the site of the ARA in response to the wish of Agrippina«. Veterans, pensioned soldiers of the legions stationed on the Rhine with their families, artisans and traders settled in COLONIA.

50—70 The CCAA is given a city wall, about 2.5 miles in length, with new gates and numerous towers. The axes of its main streets are still a decisive factor in the city of Cologne: The CARDO MAXIMUS parallel to the Rhine in a north-south direction, is the main street. The DECUMANUS MAXIMUS which runs from the Rhine to the west, is now the Schildergasse.

90 The Roman military districts on the Rhine become provinces due to an administrative reform. Now Cologne was the capital of Lower Germania. The governor resided in the PRAETORIUM.

310 For the protection of the border, Emperor Constantine orders the establishment of the Deutzer citadel on the right bank of the Rhine and has it connected with the city by a permanent bridge.

313/314 About this time, there is a Christian church on what is now the site of the cathedral. The first known bishop is Maternus.

401 The Roman legions are recalled from the Rhine frontier. Cologne comes under the rule of the Franks.

818 Hildebold, friend and adviser of Charlemagne and first archbishop of Cologne, is buried in St. Gereon.

870 On September 27, the consecration of the old cathedral takes place. The creation of the cathedral, over 295 ft. long, with an east and west choir, and two transepts was later attributed to Hildebold.

953 Bruno, the youngest brother of Emperor Otto I, becomes the archbishop of Cologne, and at the same time, the Duke of Lorraine. Thereby, the clerical and secular powers were united in the hands of the bishop of Cologne for the first time. The first expansion of the city embraces the Roman Rhine island which, by filling in the arms of the river, and the construction of a fortification, became a merchant quarter. In the center of this Rhine suburb, Bruno founded the church of St. Martin. Also, the bridge built to the Deutzer citadel by Constantine, was taken down. As a result, the people of Cologne had to cross the river by boat until the 19th century. By order of Bruno, the old cathedral was expanded to include two new side aisles. However, his special interest focused on the new building of St. Pantaleon where he was buried in 965.

972 Emperor Otto II marries the Byzantine Princess Theophanu in Rome. Archbishop Gero of Cologne made the proposal on behalf of the emperor.

991 Empress Theophanu dies in Nimwegen and is buried in the St. Pantaleon church in Cologne.

999 Heribert, close friend of Otto III, becomes archbishop. He had an imperial chapel added to the eastern transept of the cathedral. In addition, he established a Benedictine cloister in the old Deutzer citadel where he was buried in 1021.

1049 Pope Leo IX and Emperor Heinrich III visit Cologne at the same time. From this year on, there were always representatives of the pope and the emperor in the cloister of the cathedral.

1074 Archbishop Anno crushes a rebellion by the people of Cologne against him and imposes severe penalties on many residents.

1106 The second expansion of the city envelops three large cloister districts on the land side of the city which had previously lain outside the city's Roman walls.

1135 About this time, the first civic center is built on the site of the present city hall. The first city seal is added to those of the king and the archbishop. Property contracts between individual citizens are registered in the first municipal archives.

1164 On July 23, Rainald von Dassel, archbishop of Cologne and imperial chancellor to Italy, arrives in Cologne with the relics of the Three Magi which he brought from Milan.

1180 The city is expanded for the third time. By 1220, the ring wall, over five miles long, with twelve gates, was completed. It enclosed all cloister districts and large areas used for agriculture, in a broad semi-circle, beginning at the Rhine, which heretofore had not been fortified.

1247 The last of the twelve Romanesque churches which still exist today, the cloister church of St. Kunibert, is consecrated although the west tower is still under construction. During this year, the churches of other monasteries are completed: St. Gereon, St. Severin, St. Aposteln (St. Apostles), St. Georg (St. George) and St. Andreas (St. Andrew),

Martyrdom of St. Ursula with Cologne in the background, 1411 (Wallraf-Richartz-Museum)

and also the convents St. Maria im Kapitol (St. Mary in the Capitol, St. Cäcilien (St. Cecilia) and St. Ursula, and two Benedictine cloister churches, St. Pantaleon and St. Martin, and the little parish church of St. Maria Lyskirchen (St. Mary Lyskirchen).

1248 On August 15, the foundation for the Gothic cathedral is laid.

1288 During the battle of Worringen, fought between various princes because of disputes over inheritances, an important decision is made affecting the people of Cologne. Siding with the victors against the defeated Archbishop Siegfried von Westerburg, they achieve political freedom for the city. From that time on, the archbishops who, since the middle of the century had resided in Bonn, only came to Cologne on ecclesiastical occasions.

1388 The first public university in Germany is founded in Cologne.

1396 After several rebellions against the patricians who had held sole power thus far, the artisans take over city rule. On September 14, a manifesto takes effect in which the artisan guilds, united in so-called »Gaffeln«, establish a new constitution for the city.

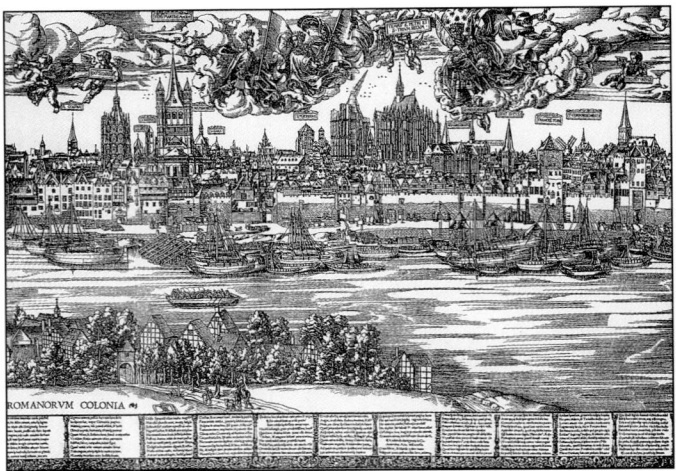

Anton Woensam: Large View of Cologne. Woodengraving in 9 parts. Cologne 1531 (section)

1414 The tower of city hall is completed. On its five floors, divided by large windows, some 130 statues placed on pedestals look down upon the city.

1424 The Jews, who can be traced in Cologne back to the 4th century and who had already settled by the mid-11th century on the land of the Roman Praetorium and were direct neighbors of city hall, are permanently banned from Cologne. On the site of the synagogue the Chapel of the City Councillors is erected. Stefan Lochner, an artist of the age, painted the famous »Altar of the City Patrons« (1445) for the chapel in the middle part of the century.

1475 Emperor Friedrich III elevates Cologne to a free imperial city with the right to mint coins.

1544 The first Jesuits arrive in Cologne and soon begin teaching at the venerated Three-Magi high school. They supported the city against the reformation which Archbishop Hermann von Wied wanted to introduce.

1560 Construction work on the cathedral is stopped. The choir, 147 ft. in interior height and completed around 1300, is separated by a wall from the long- and cross-aisles which are only 43 ft. high. The south tower is 162 ft. high, the transept façades have yet to be built.

1573 The city hall is given a Renaissance vestibule whose decorations are a reminder of the Roman past as well of the delivery from the temporal power of the archbishop.

1583 The attempt of Archbishop Gebhard Truchsess von Waldburg, to change the archbishopric of Cologne into a protestant principality, leads to the so-called Truchsessian war. Catholic princes and citizens of Cologne win the conflict with the help of Bavarian troops. Ernst von Bavaria becomes the new archbishop. He was the first of five bishops from the house of Wittelsbach.

1618 The Jesuits, strongly supported by the archbishop, begin with the construction of St. Mariä Himmelfahrt (Church of the Assumption of the Blessed Virgin).

1686 On February 23, merchant Nikolaus Gülich is beheaded. He had disclosed irregularities in the council, and with the support of many people, had effected the conviction of corrupt council members. Alas, he met his Waterloo when he abused the power which he had gained in the city during his rebellion.

1794 On October 6, the city council voluntarily turns over the keys of the city to the commander of the French Revolution forces in Cologne, sealing the fate of the free imperial city. French administration and law were introduced. The archbishopric was dissolved, the university closed.

1802 All cloisters are declared property of the state, institutions are dissolved, and the convent buildings are broken up. But at the same time, free practice of religion was guaranteed. Since the catholic congregations now transferred their divine services to the former large cloister churches, they were preserved, while most of the smaller parish churches were gradually razed because they fell into disrepair. Countless paintings, sculptures, and ecclesiastical paraphernalia were lost in spite of attempts by collectors such as Ferdinand Franz Wallraf, the brothers Sulpiz and Melchior Boissereé, who tried to save as many works of art as possible. Jews and Protestants, who for centuries had not been tolerated in the city, founded new communities.

1814 Even prior to the abdication of Napoleon who visited Cologne in 1804 and 1811, the French leave the city after 20 years. Prussian and Russian troops replace them.

1821 An agreement between Prussia and the pope restores the archbishopric of Cologne. The new archbishop Earl von Spiegel, took office in 1825. As the first bishop since the middle of the 13th century, he laid no claim to secular power and he again resided in the city.

1822 After over 300 years, a new bridge is built across the Rhine again. Others soon followed. Today Cologne has 8 bridges.

1825 The first Rhine steamer is launched. The route Cologne–Rotterdam–Antwerp has regular steamboat service.

1839 The first trains of Müngersdorf begin service on the newly finished Cologne-Aix-la-Chapelle railroad line.

1842 On September 4, in presence of King Friedrich IV of Prussia, the cornerstone is laid for the expansion of the cathedral.

1861 The Wallraf-Richartz-Museum is opened. Merchant Heinrich Richartz donated money to build the museum where extensive art collections of Ferdinand Franz Wallraf, who died in 1824, were exhibited.

1880 The cathedral is completed. Dedication services are short and unceremonious because Archbishop Melchers, who lived in Holland, had great difficulty with the Prussian state and was not allowed to be in Cologne for the occasion.

1881 Medieval fortifications that constrict the rapidly growing city are razed. Only a few remnants, among them three gates, were spared. Later, ring roads were built on the site of the old town moat, adjacent to the carefully planned new districts of Cologne.

1888 First, a number of villages on the left side of the Rhine are incorporated into the precincts of Cologne. In 1910, 1914, 1922, and 1975 the city continued expanding from less than one-half mile in the Roman era to over 155 square miles today.

1917 In the middle of World War I, Konrad Adenauer, who had already been a deputy mayor since 1906, becomes mayor of Cologne. During his term of office, the university was reopened in 1919; in 1923 the stadium in Müngersdorf was built; starting in 1924, a 4.23-mile-long inner green belt, and an 18.63 mile-long outer green belt were laid around

August Sander: The Heumarkt with the monument of Friedrich Wilhelm III. Photograph about 1935

Cologne; and lastly, the Cologne Trade Fair grounds were established on the Deutzer side of the Rhine.

1933 Adenauer is deposed after the NSDAP became the strongest party in the city council on March 13.

1939 On September 1, World War II begins.

1941 During the construction of an air-raid shelter on the south side of the cathedral choir, the Roman Dionysian mosaic is discovered. Today, it is the focal point of the Roman-Germanic Museum which opened in 1974.

1942 Josef Frings, regent of the seminary, becomes archbishop of Cologne. The city suffers its first major air raid.

1945 On March 6, the war ends for Cologne. American troops occupy the city which has been 90 percent destroyed. Adenauer resumes his post as mayor from May 4 to October 6. Later, he was the first chancellor of the Federal Repulic of Germany from 1949–63.

1948 To commemorate the laying of the cathedral cornerstone 700 years ago, Cologne celebrates a magnificent festival amid the war ruins on August 15. The choir re-opens and restoration of the nave vault is begun (finished in 1956).

Karl-Hugo Schmölz: View of the Wallrafplatz as seen from the Cologne Cathedral. Photograph 1946

1967 Konrad Adenauer dies at the age of 91, and lies in state in the cathedral.

1985 During the »Year of the Romanesque Churches«, opened by Cardinal Höffner in services in St. Maria im Kapitol, all twelve medieval churches are restored except the tower of the Kunibert church and the west transept.

1986 On September 6, the new Wallraf-Richartz-Museum/Ludwig Museum is opened. A week later, the Cologne philharmonic hall with 2,000 seats opens.

1989 The number of visitors passes one million since the opening of the new twin museums. The philharmonic hall is usually sold out for most performances. The Museum of Applied Arts, second in size only to Berlin's, opens. New buildings to house two museums in the inner city are planned: the Rautenstrauch-Joest-Ethnology Museum, and the Erzbischöfliche Diözesan-Museum (Archbishopric Diocesan Museum). With the construction of the MediaPark, a new era dawns for Cologne.

III »Economic Center-West« or: How Cologne Makes a Living

by Gerhard Knauf

The »Economic Center-West«, as Cologne likes to refer to itself, is the third largest economic area in West Germany after Munich and Stuttgart. Almost 70 billion deutschmarks are earned annually by better than 400,000 employees. Industry, trade, skilled labor, and services are the backbone of this success.

Much of this prosperity is owed to the citiy's long economic tradition. Even during the Roman era, Cologne was a trade center for various goods, English wheat and Spanish wine. All who shipped their goods through Cologne by boat were obliged to store them in the city for three days during which time the people of Cologne could execute their right of first refusal. This made Cologne the richest city of the Middle Ages. In this century, it was Henry Ford who recognized the optimal geographic position of Cologne in the heart of Europe, and erected his first European factory here. Thus, »Europe 92« is no nightmare for Cologne but is regarded by the economy and administration as a chance to bring new life into a 2,000-year-old tradition.

Readiness for innovation and investment is visible everywhere in and around Cologne. The dynamo is the chemical industry all around Cologne with approximately 70 companies, 70,000 workers, and an annual gross of over 20 billion deutschmarks. The automotive and engine-building industry, which produces goods

»The Seven Hills« (Siebengebirge): Warehouse at the Rheinauhafen in the southern part of the city (1908/09; Architect Hans Verbeek)

The Ford factory in Cologne: Building the »Fiesta«

valued at 10 billion deutschmarks, offers almost as many jobs in its 200 companies. Ford with 25,000 employees is Cologne's largest employer and major producer within the city limits. But it is the many medium- and small-sized enterprises, especially in the engine-building sector, which contribute to the economy. This highly specialized branch of industry is supplemented by 20,000 businesses in the skilled occupations sector where almost 50 guilds, encompassing about 200,000 employees and 25,000 apprenticeship positions are represented. They are accommodated by the city with 15 planned or newly built industrial and business parks.

   The principle is simple yet effective with regard to both the economy and city planning. By withdrawing industrial operations from the heart of the city, areas for redevelopment are created to benefit the population. Today, this practice is emulated all over Germany as the »Cologne Model«. Land of manageable size often close to residential areas on the fringes of the city, is fully developed. Architecturally homogeneous structures are built and made available to various businesses at favorable terms. In the middle of Cologne a most impressive example of the city's policy in urban development and economic structure is taking shape – the MediaPark. At one time a freight yard, this 200,000 square meter parcel of land, is the site of six new buildings designed by the German-Canadian urban architect Eberhard Zeidler. The buildings are grouped in a semi-circle around a central plaza. The

View of the Bayer Company in Leverkusen on the Rhine. The city limits of Cologne run through the property of the company.

resulting office space of some 120,000 square meters will be occupied by companies from the telecommunication and media branches, by training and education projects, and by research and development in these areas. Art and culture belong, insofar as they utilize new techniques, just as much to the concept as does a cinema center, shops, cafés and restaurant. In addition about 200 apartments will be built. The center for telecommunications and media will be surrounded by about 100,000 square meters of public park with a small lake. With this Cologne's reputation in urban development will be increased and its favored role as a media center enhanced. Even now, five radio and television stations, film studios, 400 publishing and printing houses and over 30,000 specialized employees are found in this industry.

With 20,000 workers and an overall income of about 15 billion deutschmarks, 60 insurance companies headquartered in Cologne and 200 branch offices of other companies contribute to the economic potential of the city as well. They make Cologne one of the largest insurance metropolises of Europe, and certainly one of the oldest, because the *collegia tenuiorum* or *collegia funeratica* of the Roman era already assured suitable burial for those who paid monthly premiums. While the old location of the insurance companies lay on the ring roads, today the tendency is growing toward removing these operations and their intensive concentration of personnel and space from the inner city, and transplanting them to either the outer part of the city or the banks of the Rhine. As a result, a series of towering buildings has been created, which have established Cologne's international reputation as a place of modern business architecture.

There are buildings of less architectural significance in the city – over 300 banks and offices, employing about 15,000 Cologne residents. The city of Cologne itself contributes not inconsiderably to the expanding economy, since it employs 23,000 officials, employees and workers, and has a budget of 3.5 billion deutschmarks. Also, the archbishopric of Cologne, with its revenue of almost 1 billion deutschmarks, presently the largest income of any archbishopric in the world, makes a significant contribution to the economy.

In Cologne, special reliance is placed upon the service sector because despite the creation of enormous wealth, industrial employees are declining in number. With about 59,000 unemployed, that is 15.9 percent in the city limits (average 1988). Cologne unemployment exceeds the average for large cities and is far above the average of the country which at present is just under 10 percent. City council and administration are trying in every way possible to counteract the situation and a specially created office for economic promotion makes great efforts to attract investors.

Special success was achieved in the hotel business. Around ten new hotels were, or are being erected, half in the luxury class. They supplement the 12,000 beds in hotels, boarding houses and guest houses which Cologne already provides, and in which annually, 1,000,000 tourists stay at least two nights. If one adds all those who stay in the homes of friends and relatives, one arrives at the impressive number of 20 million visitors annually. This too, is an economic factor that is not to be underrated. Not only do approximately 15,400 employees in the restaurant business (Cologne has 2,670 pubs, restaurants, bars and discotheques) take great pains to accommodate guests, but so do the nearly 15,000 stores which enjoy a turnover of about 15 billion deutschmarks.

In order to make Cologne even more accessible, ten turnpikes which surround it are constantly maintained at peak condition and the airport which handles 120,000 tons of freight annually and is second only to Frankfurt, is being expanded. Furthermore, a magnetically-driven rapid transit system to the airport is in the planning stage. The long overdue connection with Düsseldorf and Frankfurt airports will be established and strengthen Cologne's role as the most important traffic junction in the west-

Hyatt Regency Hotel at the Deutzer Rhine Bank

ern part of the country. Daily, around 800 passenger trains leave the main train station of Cologne, one to two minutes apart, thus making it the most heavily used in the Federal Republic. This position is further reinforced by 250 freight trains that daily cross the Südbrücke (South Bridge), contributing to the 25 million tons of rail freight that are annually shipped through the newly constructed container facility as well as the old freight yards. It comes as no surprise that under these circumstances, the city is eager to be tied into the planned high-speed, route to Paris so the »Economic Center-West« can give and receive more impetus within a united Europe.

IV Two Art Quarters at Your Service!
The Art Scene in Cologne

by Christiane Vielhaber

Who says you cannot have everything? Anyone who comes to Cologne for art finds a cornucopia there. Yet making the right selection from among a profusion of attractions in the galleries and at art dealers is indeed an art. Cologne is one of the most attractive cities in Europe with respect to contemporary art which, besides the permanent collection in the Ludwig Museum, can be found in the more than 60 galleries. Since it is an inherent part of the gallery business to change their exhibits every few weeks, it is absolutely impossible to provide an accurate program of what is available at any one time. This is compounded by the fact that the life span of new galleries cannot be predicted! But what does not change is the hard core of Cologne's art scene. Its concentration lies where the action is, which is most convenient. It is also an undisputed fact that there are remarkable galleries outside the city: for example, the Gmurzynska gallery in Marienburg which, in addition to master works of the international classic contemporary art, repeatedly comes out with top-notch presentations of Russian avant-garde. Its changing exhibits rank high among the museums.

During the course of the past years, two focal points have emerged in the inner city – the region around St.-Apern-Strasse, with its composite offers of galleries, art, and antique stores, and the Belgian quarter around the Venloer- and Bismarckstrasse.

An almost mandatory starting point of the first mile of art is the Walther König Buchhandlung (bookstore) at the corner of Ehrenstrasse/Albertusstrasse. Anything that was ever written about art, artists, handicraft or photography, and which is fresh off the press in catalogues or magazines – König has it! Even his »junk shop« is a paradise for browsing. Diagonally across from König's in the Gertrudenstrasse, is the Werner gallery. It is among other things the top source of works by the prominent artists Penck, Lüpertz,

Immendorff, or Baselitz. Thanks to Werner's excellent connection with the U.S. market, its changing exhibits also present top-notch artists of the U.S. scene.

St.-Apern-Strasse is probably the most varied mile of art in Cologne. Not only has Sotheby's auction house had its store and exhibition rooms but there are also galleries of contemporary art, such as the Wentzel gallery which specializes in American Color-Field-Painting. It has also made a name for itself by displaying the works of Stöhrer as well as sculptures by Caro and Kricke. Vis-à-vis, the Tengelmann gallery offers more recent yet inexpensive art. Those looking for icons and old jewelry will find them at Rotmann's. For those interested in antiques and archeological finds, a visit to Weber is an absolute must.

Before one walks through the Kreishauspassage to the Albertusstrasse, one should follow the Apernstrasse straight ahead to the Zeughausstrasse and the Römerturm (Roman Tower). There one finds the Inge Baecker gallery with its experimental artists such as Vostell; Cologne classical artists such as Schultze; as well as greats of the Cologne scene such as the Niedecken BAP-singers. This old-fashioned gallery alone is worth seeing. Dietze's art establishment specializes in pop art and art déco, and the Stolz gallery at the Römerturm concentrates upon abstract art of the 20s and 30s. From this point, it takes only a few steps to reach the Orangerie-Reinz gallery at the corner of Auf dem Berlich/Helenenstrasse. In contrast to the changing exhibitions, this is a permanent treasure chest, not only for German art after 1945, like Nay, Hoehme or Schumacher, but especially for first class surrealism of the classic moderns Miró, Chagall, Braque, or Picasso. Here, there are still places where one can browse at leisure!

The Zwirner and Reckermann galleries in Albertusstrasse, where are trends are established, are always worth a visit. That which has made the Zwirner gallery internationally famous cannot always be seen in the other changing exhibitions. The proprietor is rather active behind the scenes as an important dealer, be it top-notch works by Max Ernst or by Magritte, or for the art of Richter and Knoebel, which is in demand. However, in his exhibitions he also shows younger contemporaries, but only after they have made a name for themselves. Reckermann also has classics on his agenda: artists of the Nouveau Realism, like Klein and Rotella, and zero-masters like Uecker. However, he is especially committed to the primitives, like Virnich or Partenheimer, whose art is difficult to promote, but who, thanks to his efforts, already have risen to prominence on the scene. New on the first floor is the Heidi Reckermann gallery which is first and foremost engaged in supporting young national and international photographers. Her program has Tillmann, a newcomer in Cologne, and the Düsseldorfer Poensgen.

Photography and contemporary art also comprise a unit in the Kicken-Pauseback gallery in the Bismarckstrasse. That which Kicken offers in incunabula photography is alluring. Bismarckstrasse is a street best explored circuitously because right and left, ground level, basement level, or one flight up, or even in the courtyard – everywhere one looks, top-notch young artists show their talents. Discoveries are sure to be found if enough undisturbed time is available and the wherewithal for some spontaneous purchases – prices are still manageable. On the way back to the Venloer Strasse on the corner of Brüsseler Strasse stands the »Alcazar«, a place to eat and drink, a place which fits into its surroundings. In summer, it offers sidewalk tables for its guests – good to see and be seen!

Around the corner in Venloer Strasse is an entire structure devoted to galleries. The inside as well as the outside of the architectural cube, designed by the prominent Cologne architect and art collector Oswald Matthias Ungers, is alone worth seeing. The Hetzler gallery sets standards with programs featuring young German masters such as Kippenberger, the brothers Oehlen and Büttner as well as American favorites like Schnabel. Above are the Jablonka and Buchholz galleries. Although the latter is a newcomer among gallery proprietors, it already has a stable of important artists in addition to newcomers and novices on the scene. This quarter not only teems with galleries, but also with pubs and restaurants, where artists, gallery proprietors, and all those who want to be with it, have a ball. With its cultural programs, the Stadtgarten-Café on the corner of Venloer / Spichernstrasse will never end up on anyone's list of »out« places. Gallery owners take their artists out here or relax alone from their sales stress. Frequent guests here include such personalities as Giancarlo Apicella, who just dropped in for an espresso from his own gallery across the street (mainly Italian avant-garde).

Also classified as artists' pubs are the XX, the Brauhaus Päffgen on the Friesenstrasse, and the »Klein Köln«, once a hangout for boxers, which stays open until dawn. Or the Trattoria Toscana on the Friesenwall which is jampacked not only because of its first class cuisine. There is a lot of art drawn on the walls! The Chelsea in Lindenstrasse has made a good reputation for itself as a lodging house for artists and gallery proprietors. Its hotel rooms are tastefully furnished. Its Café Central is a favorite rendezvous. On Ehrenstrasse, one can view prominent people of the art world in the Broadway Café or the Spitz, and around the corner on Apostelnstrasse, one can often meet headliners of the art world such as Michael Werner, having a quick snack in Ezio's Bistro. One of the very best places for people who want to see and to be seen is the Alte Wartesaal (Old Waiting Room) abutting the main train station. The same applies to the disco Blue Monday. And whoever is already in the vicinity of the train station, should look for the Greve gallery on the Wallrafplatz, and the Holtmann gallery around the corner on Richartzstrasse. Greve's exhibits, constantly presenting works by Twombly, Kounellis, and Fontana, are the finest. Holtmann not only represents important Cologne artists like Klauke, Buthe, or Charly Banana, but above all, Joseph Beuys.

A quick trip into the south city is worthwhile at noon as well as in the evening. A visit to Chin's in the Im Ferkulum at Chlodwigplatz, where Jean Luc from Madagascar serves favored regular patrons exotic specialities, and where recently a bar has been installed in the cellar, is a must. Down there, eight artists, among them Wewerka, Buthe and C. O. Paeffgen, each have painted or decorated a pillar in their own, inimitable style.

Tullio on Bonner Strasse offers a more staid, and therefore a less stimulating atmosphere. The restaurant below the tradition-rich gallery, »Der Spiegel«, also has a garden terrace. In the Solferino on Marienburger Strasse, where collectors, artists, and gallery proprietors also regularly meet for dinner, one may (with much luck), get a beautiful view of the Rhine.

Anyone who merely follows this program for a start, and who is lucky enough to be accompanied by someone in-the-know, gets not only an idea as to why it is so beautiful at the Rhine, but realizes why Cologne is one of the most attractive and important art cities in Europe.

V Hotels in Cologne

Many Cologne hotels offer a great variety of package deals for fairs, weekends, New Year's Eve, carnival, etc. Information: Verkehrsamt Köln.

Our listings are categorized in the following price groups (for a double room per night):
Upper price category:
over 300 DM
Middle price category:
200–300 DM
Lower price category:
100–200 DM

Upper Price Category:

Dom-Hotel
Domkloster 2a
Tel. 2024-0
Excellent location for the past 125 years. Weekend arrangements, including sightseeing, and discounts for Cologne's main attractions.

Excelsior Hotel Ernst
Domplatz
Tel. 2701
Top-notch hotel. A traditional address for the past 125 years.

Holiday Inn Crowne Plaza
Rudolfplatz
Tel. 20950
Large hotel on the site of the old opera of Cologne. Swimming pool, sauna.

Hyatt Regency
Kennedy Ufer 2a
(Deutzer Rhine bank)
Tel. 828 1234
Beautiful location with a view of Cologne's panorama. Babysitting, airport limousine, swimming pool, sauna, whirlpool.

Hotel Inter-Continental
Helenenstr. 14
(near St.-Apern-Str., Neumarkt)
Tel. 228-0
Hotel with international standards. Central location.

Maritim
Heumarkt 20
Tel. 2027-0
Luxury hotel on the Rhine. Swimming pool.

Ramada Renaissance Hotel
Magnusstr. 20
(vicinity Friesenplatz, Ring)
Tel. 2034-0
Special theater and philharmonic service. Swimming pool, whirlpool, sauna, and solarium.

Hotel im Wasserturm
Kaygasse 2
(near Grosser Griechenmarkt)
Tel. 20080
First-class hotel in the historical water tower. Extravagant design and high quality furniture, all-round hotel service.

Hotels in Cologne

Middle Price Category:

Ascot
Hohenzollernring 95–97
(vicinity of the Kaiser-Wilhelm-Ring)
Tel. 521076
Small hotel with flair and class.

Dorint
Friesenstr. 44–46
Tel. 1614-0
One of the more recently built hotels.

Königshof
Richartzstr. 14–16
(Wallrafplatz, WDR)
Tel. 234583
Central location.

Pullman Hotel Mondial
Kurt-Hackenberg-Platz 1
(across from the philharmonic)
Tel. 20630
Changing exhibits of Cologne artists; tickets for the philharmonic.

Queens Hotel
Dürener Str. 287 (Lindenthal)
Tel. 4676-0
Quiet location in natural setting at the Stadtweiher (city park pond).

Viktoria
Worringer Str. 23
(vicinity of the northern bank of the Rhine)
Tel. 720476
Villa with turn of the century styling, protected as a monument, has an individual character.

Lower Price Category:

Altea
Severinstr. 199
(between the south side of town and the cathedral)
Tel. 201 30
Rooms with kitchenette on monthly rental.

**Astor und
Aparthotel Concorde**
Friesenwall 68–72
Tel. 235811
Special rates for long-term guests.

Rheinhotel Atrium
Karlstr. 2–10 (Rodenkirchen)
Tel. 393045
Free bicycles for Rhine tours, etc. maps and box lunches.

Hotel Rheingold
Engelbertstr. 33–35
Tel. 236331
Hotel in the vicinity of the Rudolfplatz.

Cöllner Hof
Hansaring 100
(near Ebertplatz/Eigelstein)
Tel. 122075
Good middle-class hotel.

Haus Marienburg
Robert-Heuser-Str. 3
(Marienburg)
Tel. 388497
Turn of the century-style villa in quiet surroundings.

Stapelhäuschen
Fischmarkt 1–3
Tel. 212193, 213043
Historic house in the old town.

1 | **Day 1 – Program:** Cathedral – Wallraf-Richartz-Museum/Ludwig Museum – Hohenzollernbrücke – Messeturm – Deutzer Brücke – Old Town – Gross St. Martin – Rheingarten – Cathedral

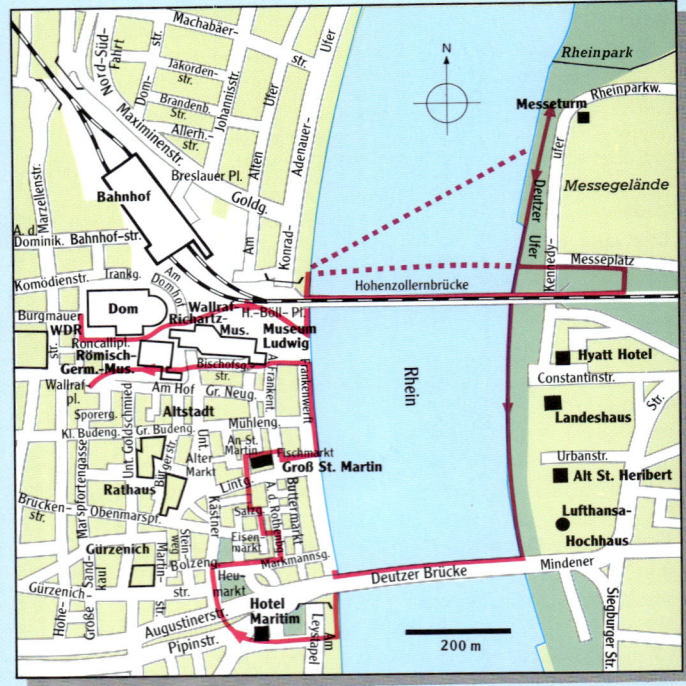

Morning — Cathedral – Wallraf-Richartz-Museum/Ludwig Museum – Hohenzollernbrücke (ferry) – Rheinpark

Lunch

Afternoon — Deutzer bank (panoramic view of Cologne's Rhine) – Deutzer Brücke – Heumarkt – Eisenmarkt – Ostermannplatz – Alter Markt – Gross St. Martin – Fischmarkt – Rheingarten – Bischofsgartenstraße – »Hafenstrasse« (reconstructed Roman street) – Cathedral

Alternatives: On Mondays, when the municipal museums are closed, visits are offered to the Archbishopric Diocesan Museum (see also »Museums«), or a walk through the culture of the Cologne art scene. (See also: »Two Art Quarters at Your Service!«, p.22)

Day 1 – Information

Café Reichard
Unter Fettenhennen 11
Daily 8:30 a.m. – 6 p.m.
Building in Neo Gothic style of 1903/04. Reconstructed in faithful detail from top to bottom; reserved place for a view of the cathedral. Sumptuous breakfast offerings ranging from *Müsli* to brunch.

Café Jansen
Corner of Obenmarspforten and Marspfortengasse
(vicinity of An Farina)
Mon–Sat 9 a.m. – 6:30 p.m., Sun 1–6 p.m., breakfast 9–12 a.m.
Old café with appealing round tower architecture.

Domplatte (Cathedral Ledge)
Steel-concrete construction of 1968–74. Architect: Fritz Schaller. Although the cathedral stands in isolation against the medieval architectural background, it has optimal impact upon the viewer. Auto traffic passes unhindered below the cathedral ledge.

Kölner Dom
(Cologne Cathedral)
Daily 6 a.m. – 7:30 p.m.; Cathedral choir, closed Sat after 1:30 p.m.; open Sun 12:30 – 4:30 p.m. only
Tours: Mon–Fri 10, 11 a.m., 2:30, 3:30 p.m.; Sat 10, 11 a.m.; Sun 2:30, 3:30 p.m. – Tower climb: 509 steps to the height of 325 feet, daily 9 a.m. – 6 p.m. during summer, open in spring and fall until 5 p.m., and until 4 p.m. in winter.

Wallraf-Richartz-Museum/ Ludwig Museum
Bischofsgartenstr. 1
Tel. 221-2379
Tues – Thurs 10 a.m. – 8 p.m., Fri–Sun 10 a.m. – 6 p.m.; Closed Mon
Open tours: Wed 6:30 p.m., Sat, Sun 11 a.m.
Cafeteria has the same hours as the museum
Opened in 1986 together with the philharmonic which is housed in the same complex. Architects: Peter Busmann and Godfrid Haberer. Creation of the Heinrich-Böll-Platz (plaza): Dani Karavan.

Hohenzollernbrücke
(Hohenzollern Bridge)
First Rhine crossing in 1855–59, then called Dombrücke (Cathedral Bridge). Reconstructed 1907–11 as the Hohenzollern bridge. Again rebuilt in 1946–48/ 1957–59 after destruction during the war. Today it is only a railroad bridge, but it is also open for pedestrians and bikers. Daily over 1,000 trains pass from Intercity to commuter trains (S-Bahn).

Left and right of the bridgeheads stand four Hohenzollern rulers on horseback: on the left bank of the Rhine, upstream: Emperor Wilhelm II, downstream: Emperor Friedrich III (1910). On the right bank of the Rhine, upstream Emperor Wilhelm I (prince regent), downstream King Friedrich Wilhelm IV (1871, 1863 respectively).

Fähre Hohenzollernbrücke – Deutzer Messe
(Hohenzollern Bridge Ferry – Deutzer Trade Fair)
Ferry operator: Hans Linden
Tel. 38 47 38, 12 16 66

Day 1 – Information

Daily from 7:30 a.m. – 7:30 p.m., departing every 5–10 minutes from Easter to about the end of October, as well as during fairs held outside the regular season.

Köln Messe (Cologne Fair)
With 38 international fairs and exhibitions, the Cologne Fair grounds are a world trading center for goods, services, and information. Nearly half of the fair themes deal with high tech and investment opportunities. Over 28,000 exhibitors from 100 countries, and 1.8 million buyers and visiting professionals from more than 150 countries participate regularly.

Messeturm Restaurant
(Fair Tower Restaurant)
Kennedy Ufer 21
(Fair Grounds)
Reservations: Tel. 88 10 08
Sun–Fri 12–3 p.m., 7–10 p.m., Sat after 7 p.m.
Restaurant 230 feet above ground level, with a beautiful view of Cologne's old town.

Rheinpark (Rhine Park)
Hours: Summer 7 a.m. – midnight; Winter 8 a.m. – dusk
Former federal garden show grounds for lovers of landscape designs and buildings of the 50s. During summer, the Tanzbrunnen (Dancing Fountain) with space for around 1,500 visitors; is a local attraction: changing open-air musical events featuring local and foreign headliners.

Hyatt Regency Hotel
Kennedy Ufer 2a
Tel. 828 12 34
In the lounge on the first floor one can savor the classic Cologne panorama.

Landschaftsverband Rheinland (Rhineland State Planning Commission)
State capitol, erected in 1957/58 by architects Ernst von Rudloff and Eckhard Schulze-Fielitz, provides for road building, clinics and museums.

Alt St. Heribert
Former Benedictine abbey within the area of the former Roman citadel, »castra divitium«. Founded in 1002 by the Archbishop Heribert. Church of the 17th century restored after World War II. (Cannot be visited.) Today, a home for old people is located in the restored abbey buildings.

Deutsche Lufthansa AG
A 19-story skyscraper (1967–70) houses its headquarters.

Deutzer Brücke
(Deutzer Bridge)
Widened in 1947/48, 1976/80. A little further north, during the 4th century, there was the Roman bridge connecting the Roman provincial capital with the citadel on the right bank of the Rhine.

Hotel Maritim
Heumarkt 20
Tel. 20 27-0
Luxury lodging house on the Rhine, 1987–89. Architects: Gottfried Böhm, Kraemer, and Sieverts. Buildings connected by

Day 1 – Information

a glass gallery. Café with a view of the Rhine.

Heumarkt (Hay Market)
During the Middle Ages a splendid market, but not so today. The stock exchange building, erected in 1730, was extensively damaged during the war. Presently, the Heumarktdenkmal (Hay Market Monument), featuring the Prussian King Friedrich Wilhelm III and surrounded by important figures in Prussian history, is under construction. In 1878 it was erected by the city in honor of the then Prussian government. A bright future is anticipated for the »plaza«: that which the Cologne ring roads have already accomplished, the so-called beautifying »restoration« is also in store for the Heumarkt.

Ostermannbrunnen
(Ostermann Fountain)
Ostermannplatz
After the completion of the old town restoration, it was erected by carnival devotees in 1939 on the former Heumarkt, in memory of the author of many famous Cologne folk and carnival songs, Willi Ostermann. The fountain figures represent characters in his songs: »*et Schmitze Billa*« (according to the song, she had a villa in Poppelsdorf), »*de Tant*« (the Aunt), »*kölsche Mädcher*« (Cologne Girls), and »*de Funkesoldat*« (The militiaman).

An Gross St. Martin
At the north side of the church is the prize-winning new building complex with dwellings and stores, erected in 1975–78 by J. Schürmann. Bronze figure of the Holy Martin by Elmar Hillebrand.

Alter Markt (Old Market)
Market place of the Middle Ages and center of the present old town. Among others, the Renaissance duplex »Zur Brezel-Zum Dorn«, (No.20/22), which has a quaint Cologne pub on the first floor, is worth seeing. Opposite it, under the face of the city hall tower clock, is the »Platz-Jabbeck«, a large head with a black hat which opens its mouth *(»Jabbeck«)* each time the clock strikes the hour (15th century).

Sited on the market place, the **Jan-van-Werth-Brunnen** (fountain), was built in 1884 in memory of the cavalry General Jan van Werth (1593–1652) during the Thirty Years War. The »Story of Jan and Griet«, depicted on two lateral reliefs, has a firm place in Cologne lore as well as in the carnival. The story is re-enacted annually in front of the Severinstor.

The servant Jan of the Cologne Kümpchenshof goes to war because the maid Griet rejects his love since he is too poor. He returns as a successful general. Griet, who is still selling apples on the market, is very sorry that she had given him the brush-off. Alas, her change of mind comes too late. The reunion supposedly took place in the classic dialogue, »*Jan, wer et haett jewoss!*« (Jan, who could have known!). »*Jriet, wer et haett jedonn!*« (Griet, who could have done it.).

Day 1 – Information

Gross St. Martin
(Church of St. Martin)
Martinspförtchen 8
Hours: Mon-Fri 10 a.m. – 6 p.m.,
Sat 10 a.m. – 12:30 p.m., 1:30 – 6
p.m., Sun and holidays 2–4 p.m.
Romanesque church erected on
the ground of Roman camps, built
in the 10th century. After the city
fire in 1150, it was re-built in its
present shape during the 13th
century. Only Cologne church
where murals of the 19th century
are preserved.

Robert-Blum-Plaque
In Mauthgasse 9, at the foot of
Gross St. Martin, once stood the
birthplace of the freedom fighter
Robert Blum (1807–48).

Stapelhäuschen
Fischmarkt 1–3
Tel. 21 21 93, 21 30 43
Restaurant (also open-air café)
and hotel
Medieval house where the hoisting equipment that used to lift
wares to the upper floors of the
storehouse can be seen.

Campi
Am Frankenturm/
corner Bischofsgartenstr.
Daily 8 a.m. – midnight
Italian café, bar, snacks.

Heinzelmännchenbrunnen
(Fountain of Elves)
Erected in 1899 in memory of the
author August Kopisch, who
wrote the saga of the Cologne's
elves.

Früh am Dom
Am Hof 12–14
Daily 10 a.m. – midnight
One of Cologne's tradition-rich
breweries, Kölsch on tap, and
specialties of Cologne.

Café Sagui
Am Hof/Hohe Str. 164–168
Daily 10 a.m. – 11 p.m.
Italian ice cream parlor.

Köbes with Kölschkranz at »Päffgen« in the Friesenstrasse

Between the Cathedral and the River:
The Heart of Cologne

A Madonna at the foot of the cathedral, but also at one's own? Yes, this can happen in Cologne. Because sidewalk painters, by nature not very fussy in their choice of subjects, now and then copy Stefan Lochner's famous portrait of the Madonna which hangs in the cathedral, on the cathedral ledge, using colored chalk.

Madonnas in oil and chalk – something for everbody. People look to the ground and crane their necks to the towers – here the fleeting image of saint for the delight of strollers, there the black cathedral for the glory of God. Cologne has room for both, especially here, in front of the main entrance to the cathedral.

Although it was completed in its present form only three generations ago, the **Cologne Cathedral** is not just the most famous building in the city but according to informed opinion it is, on the whole, the most widely known architectural monument of Germany. When the first European parliament needed a montage featuring landmarks of European capitals, it was only logical that

Whether Rembrandt or Lochner: the sidewalk painters around the cathedral are uninhibited in their choice of subjects.

Stefan Lochner: Altar of the City Patrons, 1445 (center part). When the altar is opened up, it is 17.1 ft. wide and 9.25 ft. high. Set in place in 1809.

the press promoted a Rhine panorama dominated by the cathedral. On the other hand, the cathedral, a German landmark, has a structure that was incomplete since the late Middle Ages. It was completed during the past century as result of a surge of romantic-national enthusiasm. It is also rightly regarded as the most authentic of Gothic cathedrals although its form was developed in France.

When Master Gerhard, the first cathedral master architect, began the realization of his magnificent design around the middle of the 13th century, native construction workers, schooled in the building of Romanesque churches, were hardly suited for the completely new technical requirements. Six centuries later, the situation was reversed. At that time, one used the most modern technical devices such as a steam engine for hoisting loads to erect the majestic twin-tower façade exactly according to the medieval parchment plan which had been lost through fantastic misadventure and was later re-discovered.

Today, the Johanneskapelle (Chapel of John) of the cathedral houses the largest architectural drawing of the Middle Ages, which by the way, was the first to envision the daring use of filigree construction in the spires. The perfection of this architectural drawing, even in its details, is evident in the drawings of the 26 feet high finial, a copy of which stands in front of the west façade of the cathedral. The present cathedral master architect Arnold Wolff states, »According to the original medieval plan, the two finials on the towers were supposed to have a total height of about 16.5 feet. Cathedral master builder Richard Voigtel considered them too tall, so he first reduced them to 15.9 feet as shown on several working plans. Finally, they were again reduced to 15 feet, probably because of technical reasons. The revisions also affected the spaces between the leaves. They had become too thick. This was only noticed from below after the scaffolding was removed. So Voigtel had the individual leaves made thinner, thus enlarging the respective spaces between them. The finials were restored to the lightness which is evident on the parchment plan.«

In any case, the main façade with its three portals of which only the one on the right, the so-called »Petersportal« (Portal of Peter), had been completed during the Middle Ages – which fronts the five-aisle building in an ingeneous manner, corresponds to a great extent to the original plans. In contrast, the façades of the transepts had to be designed anew, since none of the medieval plans were available. When construction work came to a halt in 1560, only the choir had been completed, the south façade tower was two stories high, and the remaining aisle, at about the height of the capital area, temporarily roofed. The south façade of the transept, created by Ernst Friedrich Zwirner, the most important cathedral architect of the 19th century, is acknowledged as a masterpiece of Gothic Revival. Incidentally, after World War II, the doors of the south façade were designed by Ewald Mataré whose pupil Joseph Beuys also made a contribution to their creation. The façade of the north transept, facing the train station, was also designed by Zwirner. It was restored after having been heavily damaged during the war. It is a contemporary work. In all essential details it follows the original but allows for the creative talents of today's artisans.

Anyone glancing over the multiplicity of spires, arches, and ornamental traceries of the cathedral's pillars and flying-buttresses may at first find it somewhat confusing but at the same time impressive. One may often discover damaged spots but under close scrutiny, many parts that have already been replaced. The stone pillars and flying-buttresses support the enormous weight of the vault and roof, making possible the openings in the transept walls for the windows which are so necessary for experiencing the sense of space of the Gothic. There is a constant threat of decomposition due to the elements which because of the high degree of air pollution today, seriously threatens any filigreed structure such as the Cologne Cathedral.

On the first visit, it is a good idea to enter the Cologne Cathedral through its main entrance in the west. The interior inevitably captivates even those who are only somewhat sensitive to the thrill of spaciousness. The sweeping heights of this architecture, combined with a feeling of being drawn into depths, is a rhythm delicately emphasized by the finely delineated pillars, from which one cannot withdraw one's eyes. Walking from the center of the transept through its side aisles, this first impression is increased by an abundance of fascinating views which – not quite unjustly – the Romanticists compared to a forest full of trees.

The rich furnishings of the cathedral are primarily concentrated in the choir which alone stems from the Middle Ages; here indeed is a quality of richness and completeness which can hardly be found anyplace else.

The Cathedral of Cologne: View from the choir into transept which was completed in 1863

Front of the Shrine of the Three Magi. In the lower part on the left, the Adoration of the Three Magi, and the Baptism of Christ on the right. Mary and Child are enthroned in the center. Above the removable plate in the upper pediment, the presentation of Christ's return for the Last Judgment

In the **high choir**, the fantastically carved choir pews, the unique tempera on the choir screens, the extremely elegant figures crowned by canopies on the choir pillars, the angels (19th century) in the arcade spandrels, and finally the recently restored glass paintings of the upper clerestory, form a concise multi-tiered, interrelated ensemble. It also includes the grandiose high altar-mensa with its white marble figures carved in relief.

Behind the high altar stands the **Shrine of the Three Magi**. It is not only the largest gold relic shrine of the Middle Ages, but one of the most important works of occidental goldsmith art. One only has to look once at the impressive heads of the prophets at the lower sides of the shrine, their dramatic gestures, to get an idea of the supreme artistic talents of master Nikolaus of Verdun. It is from him that these figures, and probably the total concept of the shrine, are derived. But he did not live to see the completion of the shrine.

The relics of the Three Magi in the shrine were brought to Cologne from the conquered Milan on July 23, 1164, by Archbishop Rainald von Dassel, chancellor of Friedrich Barbarossa. They were not only the motivation for the creation of this shrine, but also for the new construction of the cathedral. By possessing the relics of the Three Magi, Cologne after Jerusalem, Rome, and

Santiago de Compostela, became a foremost stopping place for pilgrims in the Middle Ages when people believed in relics. The passage around the choir and the attached chapels contain not just an abundance of art treasures but numerous **sepulchers** of archbishops of the 10th through the 15th centuries. The development in medieval tomb sculpture can be clearly seen here. The sepulcher of Philipp von Heinsberg is especially intriguing because it is shaped like merlons on a medieval city wall. It is reminiscent of the structure that encircled Cologne during the Staufen era that this archbishop first rejected but later allowed to be built.

Even the hurried visitor should not miss two precious items: the **Gero Crucifix** on the north side of the passage around the choir. It is the oldest remaining, large piece of sculpture from the late 10th century. And, on the south side of the passage, the masterpiece of the Cologne School of Painters – the **Altar of the City Patrons**. The name of its creator has been handed down as that of Stefan Lochner, a fact that was mentioned by Albrecht Dürer in his notes.

One actually never really leaves the cathedral. One way or another, it remains present in the outer or inner eye – as a medieval façade seen from the inside of the Wallraf–Richartz-Museum, or as dominating landmark, or else as an orientation point on a walk through the city.

The route first passes the maintenance shed of the cathedral which can be seen into from above. Fifty-six stonemasons as well as other craftsmen and 18 building maintenance workers and administration personnel work to remove damaged parts of the cathedral and replace them with a more resistant stone. There they stand, the weather-beaten stones and the corroded small Gothic spires of a cathedral which never was, nor will be, completed. If the environmental pollution continues its erosion, present cathedral master architect Arnolf Wolff fears that one day not one of the original stones will remain and in plain English, that the Cologne Cathedral gradually will become merely a copy of itself, more or less fit for export to Disneyland.

At the cathedral choir, on the way to the Wallraf-Richartz-Museum/Ludwig Museum, one gets a look at the recently glazed hall of the **Hauptbahnhof** (Main Train Station). What a spacial trinity of buildings as a witness to faith in a Greater Being – a heavenly, a technological, and an artistic power! A Gothic cathedral, a technical feat, and a modern art palace gathered in one small area – rarely has a city developed so much sensitivity for architectural coincidence.

Cologne Cathedral choir from the east. Construction of the choir chapels began in 1248, the upper clerestory was completed around 1300.

The third and youngest of the architectural groups is the **museum complex**. Fortunately, the gigantic new construction, despite its ambitiousness, does not seek to compete with the architecture of the cathedral but skillfully blends itself into the surroundings and into the picture of the prominent Rhine panorama. The sensitively-designed Heinrich-Böll-Platz (plaza) between the two sections of the museum, under which the daringly-constructed philharmonic hall hides, belongs beyond a doubt among the most beautiful areas in Cologne, a city that indeed can boast of very few such locations.

Tom Wesselmann, Great American Nude, 1967 (Ludwig Museum)

Wallraf-Richartz-Museum/Ludwig Museum: Complete view from the Rhine. Architects: BDA Peter Busmann and Godfrid Haberer (1986)

The interior of the double museum is surprising. Sometimes, it vacillates abruptly between a grand gesture like the gala staircase in the spacious entrance hall that reminds one of Baroque times (it leads to a mere attic) to poorly or completely unresolved minor details that indicate plain narrow-mindedness. Both, the grand gesture and the pettiness, can definitely be interpreted as facets of the local mentality. That is what gives the atmosphere of this city its inimitable, but in now way disagreeable identity. In this sense, the museum, constructed by Cologne architects, is a genuine product of Cologne.

The two art collections united under one roof, the **Wallraf-Richartz-Museum** and the 20th century oriented Ludwig Museum, could also be regarded as a kind of Cologne pinacotheca.

To recommend a few for a closer look among the abundance of paintings hanging closely together here (still only a relatively

Concert Hall of the Philharmonic. Architects: BDA Peter Busmann and Godfrid Haberer with the artist Barna v. Sartory

small part of the total inventory) resembles the famous search for a needle in the haystack. Helpful is the floor plan of each individual section that is sold as the admission ticket.

It is suggested that one picks up the thread by viewing two further works by Lochner, this unique master of the Cologne School of Painters, whose name is already known: the portrayal of the »**Day of Judgment**« and the famous »**Madonna in the Rose Bower**«. Thoughtful symbolism, fastidious realism, and that inimitable Cologne charm unite in a world-renowned work of art.

The core of the museum, and also space-wise most beautifully located on the mezzanine, is the extensive collection of works of the **Cologne School of Painters**. It contains two paintings by Stefan Lochner. The two altar pieces with their side wings and wainscotted pictures from sometime late in the Middle Ages, which according to art histories are regularly attributed to different masters, are of definitely diverse qualities. But all of them are more or less marked by this unique mixture occasionally slipping into the coarsely drastic presentation of enjoyment, wrongly labeled today as a naive, pleasing, enthusiastic piety, which on one hand fascinates us with the picture world of the Middle Ages, but which, on the other hand, makes it difficult for us to understand it.

Anyone who takes a close look will find in the background of some of the legends about saints, especially the one about the Cologne city patroness Ursula the more or less distinctly recognizable city of »Holy Cologne«, girded by a wall, and with numerous churches and the uncompleted cathedral.

Another exquisite collection is that of **Dutch and Flemish paintings of the 17th century** whose spectrum runs from the programmatic »**Self-portrait Amid the Circle of Mantua Friends**« by the young **Peter Paul Rubens,** to the enigmatically-smiling **self-portrait** of the old **Rembrandt**; from the mythological scenes of the Italian trained Maerten van Heemskerck, to the similarly symbol-laden still life of Pieter Aertsen; from preciously elegant interiors by Pieter de Hooch, to the manifold landscape portrayals of Joos de Momper, Paul Bil, Jan van Goyen, or Jacob van Ruisdael.

Although in comparison to the wealth of the Dutch-Flemish paintings the collection of Italian, French, and Spanish works is much smaller, it too, contains treasures. For example, the wrongfully ignored picture of »**Emperor Augustus and the Sibyl of Tibur**«, a model example of Renaissance painting by **Benvenuto Tisi da Garofalo**, who was influenced by Raffael. »**The Rural Walk**« by the Venetian **Giovanni Battista Piazzetta** can be placed at

Flight of Stairs in the Wallraf-Richartz-Museum/Ludwig Museum. Architects: BDA Peter Busmann and Godfrid Haberer

its side as a not more inferior example of the Baroque era. And who would not be enthralled by **François Boucher's** captivating »Girl in Repose«?

Also important is the section for **19th century paintings** where the German Romantic Caspar David Friedrich, the French Realist Gustave Courbet, the Belgian James Ensor, or the Norwegian Edvard Munch are represented. The Wallraf-Richartz-Museum with the »**Sisley Couple**« by Impressionist **Auguste Renoir**, and a version of the »**Drawbridge of Arles**« by **Vincent van Gogh** has only one work each of these famous artists, a fact that is duly celebrated. However, it possesses no fewer that 32 paintings and many more graphics by **Wilhelm Leibl**, a painter who is a native of Cologne.

Finally, without resorting to the notorious Baedecker »star technique« attention is invited to an outstanding picture which naturally is missed by no pertinent guide but which unfortunately attains no effect in its narrow, dark room – **Albrecht Dürer's »Fifer and Drummer«**. It is a part of the so-called »Jabach-Altar«, having once been in the Jabach court in Cologne. Its other two parts are in museums in Frankfurt and Munich.

The **Ludwig Museum** on the floors above and below the Wallraf-Richartz-Museum has more space for exhibitions. It owes its international fame primarily to the collection of North American art of recent decades, but also it possesses a superior collection of German Expressionists. There is barely a noted artist of the 20th century who does not have at least one piece of work there. It is therefore difficult to single out names.

However, it can be claimed that **August Macke's »Lady in a Green Jacket«**, **Paul Klee's »Main Roads and Side Roads«**, **Salvador Dali's »Train Station of Perpignan«**, **Jasper John's »World Map«**, or **Edward Kienholz' »Portable War Memorial«** are among the best works of these artists while Pablo Picasso or Joseph Beuys are represented by less compelling works. By contrast Max Beckmann and Ernst Wilhelm Nay are represented in the Ludwig Museum with a series of outstanding works, as is **Max Ernst**, whose recently-acquired painting, **»The Virgin Reprimands the Christ Child in Front of Three Witnesses«**, is without a doubt one of the most brilliant works exhibited here – certainly more amusing than the museum's obviously preferred giant paintings by Penck, Georg Baselitz, or Markus Lüpertz, whose lasting qualities are yet to be proven.

A breath of fresh air feels good after intensive indulgence in art – and one can always get that at the Rhine. From the **Heinrich-Böll-Platz** one comes to the **Hohenzollern bridge**, one of the busiest and ever vibrating railroad bridges in Europe. It was recently widened but still kept its characteristic shape. From here one has an excellent view of the museum complex with the appealing **»Rhine Garden Sculpture«** by Eduardo Paolozzi, and especially, of the grandiose choir spires of the cathedral to which the bridge leads but not by chance. During the argument about the location of the Cologne railroad bridge, the romantic-minded King Friedrich Wilhelm IV personally decided to have it cross the Rhine »in the direction of the long axis of the Cologne Cathedral«.

This made it possible to have the main train station placed directly at the foot of the cathedral which was unfavorable with regard to traffic but in the tension-laden juxtaposition of divine and profane and of art and technology, was the fulfillment of characteristic ideas of the 19th century.

Unfortunately, the easy and direct way across this bridge is presently blocked because of restoration work. Therefore, one must pass the Paolozzi-Brunnen (Paolozzi Fountain), go through the Rhine garden to the river and ascend the bridge on the down-

Railroad waiting room of Cologne's Main Train Station (1890–94)

View of the Rhine to the south. In the foreground, the Romanesque St. Kunibert Church. Behind it, the Hohenzollern, Deutzer, Severin, South, and Rodenkirchener Autobahnbrücke (Turnpike Bridges)

stream side. There, a small path for pedestrians and bikers leads to the other bank.

Anyone who finds this to be too troublesome, especially since the view of the old town is blocked by iron arches, can instead make use of an original typically Cologne means of transportation – the ferry at the foot of the bridge.

Although the swaying boat ride lasts only a few minutes, a breath of short-lived romanticism floats over the excursion. On such occasions, connoisseurs of Cologne like to be reminded of the »*Müllemer Bötchen*«, an imaginary Rhine boat, celebrated in a song and on which one always – how could it be otherwise in Cologne – is in the best of spirits and gets into a carnival mood.

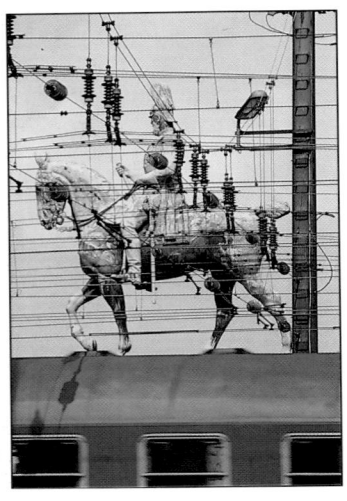

Statue of Emperor Friedrich III under the power lines of the Federal Railroad at the approach to the Hohenzollern Bridge

Cologne Fair close to Hohenzollern Bridge with the Fair Tower (1926–28; Architect: Adolf Abel) ▶

The boat docks at the **fair halls**, while the road across the bridge ends in front of their main entrance from where it is only a few steps downstream.

When in 1922, at the initiative of the then Mayor Konrad Adenauer, the Cologne Fair Association was founded, it could call upon a long tradition going back to a prerogative granted in 1360. The architectural complex, which during the course of years has been continually expanded, is basically made up of three exhibition halls, designed by Adolf Abel and arranged in a horseshoe shape. Their functional brick façades are typical examples of the Expressionistic architectural design of the 20s.

From the 262.6 feet high **Messeturm** (Fair Tower), which stands in impressive contrast to the long rows of relatively low exhibition halls, Oskar Kokoschka, in 1956, painted his brilliantly colored »View of the City of Cologne«. It can be seen in the Ludwig Museum. If not picturesquely aesthetic, the splendid view from up there can definitely have a stimulating effect on one's culinary instincts. It's time for a quick snack at the halfway point of the tour around town.

The »*Schäl Sick*«, (the sequestered, hidden side) as the people of Cologne jokingly call the right bank of the Rhine, is a fine place for strolling, a fact that more than makes up for the neglect shown towards it by city planners. The distant, yet amiable-looking granite and glass façade of the post-modern **Hyatt Regency Hotel**, the functional and austere but at the same time anxiety-full shapes of the 1950s seen in the building of the Rhineland State Planning Commission, **St. Heribert**, or the martial Cavalry statues in front of the **Lufthansa** administration building – none of them can really damage this vision.

It seems to be that one first has to leave Cologne to get an overall impression of the city. And, Deutz is likewise a vantage-point for the best view of Cologne's panorama.

Understandably, this typical view from across the Rhine was also that chosen for the earliest depictions of the city. In earlier times the great city wall could be seen in the foreground behind which a confusion of houses with many churches arose. Most of these churches have disappeared since then but the towers of St. Severin in the south, the city hall tower, and above everything, the mighty tower of Gross St. Martin, and naturally, the dominating cathedral still mark the best of Cologne today. Cologne is without a doubt one of the most picturesque cities in Europe. Even the effects of the seemingly out-of-place buildings like the telephone company skyscraper on the Nord-Süd-Fahrt, or the WDR sky-scraper do little to detract from its image.

Along the river, even more so going back across the **Deutzer bridge**, one's own progress produces a regular tour of the hori-

Atrium of the Maritim Hotel at the Heumarkt (1987–89; Architects: Gottfried Böhm, Kraemer, and Sieverts)

zon: the vertical hierarchy of the churches does remain but one tower pushes itself in front the next only to disappear behind it and then reappear.

From the bank of the river one could slip directly into the old town via the first spiral staircase, through Markmannsgasse and Auf dem Rothenberg – were it not for the **Hotel Maritim** which deserves some attention, too. To get to its main entrance at the Heumarkt (Hay Market), one must go under the bridge and around the building. The functional building is at present the most recent in a chain of hotel buildings which Cologne, with its growing attractiveness, not only wishes to have but actually encourages. The heart of this gigantic building of beds is undoubtedly the brilliantly-lit glass lobby, truly Texan in proportion, and which stands in soothing contrast to the usual faintheartedness of Cologne as seen in many other places. The purpose of this glass spaceship which seems to glide through the two hotel blocks on either side, is as clear as its shiny granite floor. Hotel guests and trade fair visitors should not if possible even leave this well-regulated artificial universe because not only can they sleep here but they can meet, eat, drink, take a walk or shop. The real world outside the door? No thank you! Understandable, at least here because the Heumarkt ist surely one of the most messed up places in Cologne. Yet, one could speculate that the Maritim might be the first phase leading towards the gradual redemption of the once so highly praised Heumarkt.

For starters, a quick glance before the tour through the **old town** begins is sufficient because for the time being, there will be no more panoramic views and wide perspectives. Instead, the eye is confined to narrow spaces, small places, courtyards, and twisting alleyways.

As stated, the entrance is via the cobblestone pavement alleyway Auf dem Rothenberg (at Markmannsgasse) where, by the corner of a house, a bronze figure points to the Cologne puppet theater. The first passage between the houses leads, after a few feet, left to a little plaza, the **Eisenmarkt** (Iron Market). This is the first of an enticing trilogy of peaceful inner courts, surrounded by narrow house fronts, connected by small and nameless alleys and arches. After crossing the Salzgasse, one enters the **Ostermannplatz** with its fountain named after Ostermann, a beloved song composer. Finally, one arrives at the inner court **An Gross St.**

1

Martin where the bronze figures by Wolfgang Reuter of Tünnes and Schäl, mascots of Cologne humor, stand.

It was certainly a lucky circumstance for the local architectural environment that Joachim Schürmann, the architect responsible for the restoration of Gross St. Martin (Church of St. Martin), was also permitted to design the new buildings around the church. By following part of the old plans of the cloister, he created a completely contemporary architecture in 1975–78, yet preserved the proportions of the old Martin quarter.

At the end of Brigittengässchen at the Gothic Martinspförtchen (built in 1215, later relocated here) appears a view of the **Alter Markt** (Old Market) – the city hall tower opposite the old Jan-van-Werth-Brunnen (fountain). Each year, on the Thursday preeceeding carnival, at 11:11 a.m., all hell breaks loose here because on this day, the women of Cologne take over the reign of merrymaking. From here at the Alter Markt for three wild days this city is in its glory.

The attractive tower of **Gross St. Martin** which once was higher than the cathedral's before its completion, is still an outstanding feature of the Cologne Rhine panorama today. The slender corner towers, crowned by pleated roofs, give this mighty cross tower above the three-conch design (typical of Cologne) its unmistakeable character. The structure of the building is relatively plain, but

Cologne Street Carnival: On Shrove Thursday the women take over City Hall and merrymakers rule the streets.

Idyll in the Rheingarten: the Fischmarkt at Gross St. Martin

the cloverleaf-shaped choir which faces the Rhine is rather elaborate. Art historians coined the phrase »Chorfassade« (choir façade) as an expression of their concern about the impact of other construction around it.

The interior of the former Benedictine abbey church, whose severe war damage was repaired only a few years ago, surprises one with an amazing brightness – primarily the result of the lack of the original colored glass windows. At times, it was compared to the aesthetics of an empty building site but at the same time it offered the supreme elegance of the architecture. Especially it was a chance for viewing the interior of the choir without obstruction. The remainder of the 19th century interior coloring had accidently been left untouched and preserved only by chance. In conjunction with the quietly elegant new lighting fixtures, it creates a very sensitive, perhaps even somewhat modest setting for perception of monuments, which is diametrically opposite to the self-assured decorative cheerfulness in St. Gereon.

Many people in Cologne do not even know that Gross St. Martin is the parish church of the city's Portuguese community. Near the choir, a small staircase leads down to the Rhine, and on the right to the **Fischmarkt** (Fish Market), the area in front of the »Stapelhäuschen« (Store House). Here begins a picture-book Cologne, a Cologne which would lend itself to a stage setting. Here, the mighty choir section of Gross St. Martin towers over the pleasing idyll of restored half-timbered and gabled buildings. No wonder the »Kölsch« tastes especially good here, above all during the summer, when the alleys of the old town, freed of car traffic, change into a humming beer and wine garden.

This picture of a leisurely romantic city, reminiscent of Spitzweg (a German Norman Rockwell), has not always existed. For a long time, Cologne's old town had such a bad reputation that during the 30s, a housecleaning was in order. As J. R. Beines, the city conservator stated, »This quarter ... has gone to seed since the end of the 19th century. After the removal of the city wall (1881), many of the families who had traditionally made their home there preferred to reside near the rings or in the general vicinity of the new city. Also many businesses felt too confined in the quarter and moved out. In their stead, more and more questionable gastronomic enterprises concentrated in St. Martin's quarter. The quality of the historical architecture deteriorated visibly.« The restoration report of 1938 clearly states the nationalsocialistic rationale: »The objective, besides the rescue of historic building quality, was the settling of a »better« class of people in this quarter.«

The way to the Rhine is now clear thanks to the river bank tunnel which made the green Rhine garden possible – a blessing of municipal construction, which does not exactly come to Cologne very often. Cologne on the Rhine – here it has it all – for the idle stroller who knows how to treasure walks along the bank; for the hungry, who use it as a picnic site during summer; for the biker, or for ordinary people who simply want to sit in the sun. Mother Colonia and Father Rhine entered into a rare, happy marriage in this municipal oasis.

The walking tour comes gradually to its end. Shortly before the restless Paolozzi fountain, Bischofsgartenstrasse leads past the

Gross St. Martin seen from the north-west

museum towards the cathedral. Parallel to it, the so-called **Hafenstrasse**, does the same. This reconstruction of a Roman street, with authentic cut stones, bumpy and jolty, and not at all for high heels, forecasts the theme of tomorrow's program of the day. It is here at the latest that some may feel that certain chapters from the 2.000-year-old history of Cologne, which so far kept the mind occupied, have slipped down to one's feet.

What would then be better than a relaxing rest somewhere close by? That the stimulating present and the significant past of

Heinzelmännchenbrunnen – the Fountain of Elves

Cologne are united together is evident at **Heinzelmännchenbrunnen** (Fountain of Elves). Over an occasional glass of Kölsch beer or Cappucino, the Spanish-green stones of the fountain relate one more Cologne legend. Once, the elves tumbled down the stairs to escape the curiosity of the tailor's wife. Too bad. Ever since, the people of Cologne have had to do their own work. (As the story goes, the little men, *Heinzelmännchen,* once did all kinds of chores for people prior to the incident of the nosey tailor's wife.)

Corpus Christi Procession in front of the Cologne Cathedral

Day 2 – Program: Römisch-Germanisches Museum – Praetorium – Rathaus – Gürzenich – St. Maria im Kapitol – Schildergasse – Olivandenhof – Neumarkt – St. Aposteln – Mittelstrasse – Pfeilstrasse – Friesenviertel – St. Gereon – Römerturm – Stadtmuseum – St. Andreas

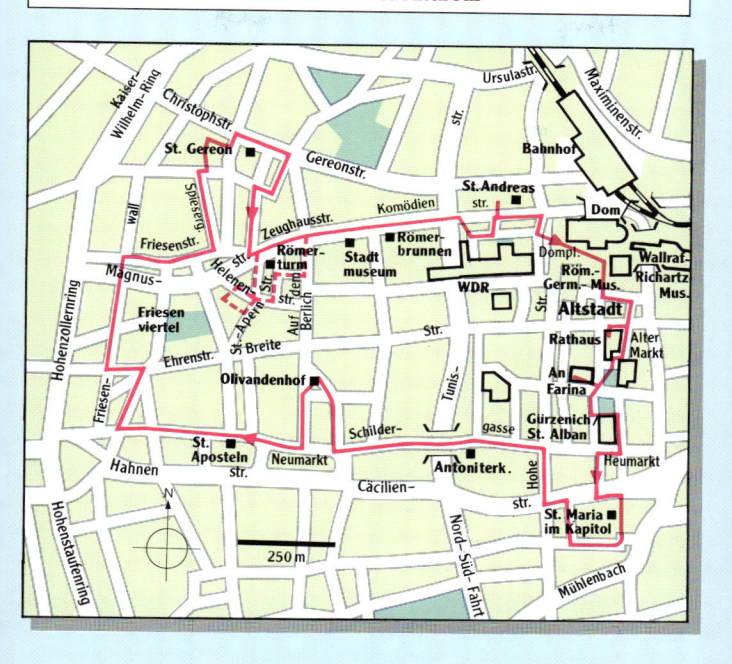

Morning — Tour through the Römisch-Germanische Museum – Praetorium – Rathaus – An Farina – Gürzenich/St. Alban – St. Maria im Kapitol – Hohe Strasse – Schildergasse – Antoniterkirche – Olivandenhof – Neumarkt Passage – St. Aposteln

Noon — Snack in the Olivandenhof, in the Neumarkt Passage, in the Bazaar de Cologne, or (a little later) in the Friesenstrasse

Afternoon — Mittelstrasse – Pfeilstrasse – Ehrenstrasse – Friesenwall – Friesenstrasse – St. Gereon – Römerturm – St.-Apern-Strasse/Kreishausgalerie – Römermauer – Stadtmuseum – Römerbrunnen – St. Andreas – Cathedral forecourt

Alternatives: Compare with Day 1

Day 2 – Information

Römisch-Germanisches Museum
(Roman-Germanic Museum)
Roncalliplatz 4
Tues, Fri–Sat 10 a.m.–5 p.m.,
Wed, Thurs 10 a.m.–8 p.m.;
Closed Mon
Public tours: Sun 11:30 a.m.
History of Roman art and culture.

Shell goblet of the 4th century A.D.

Praetorium
Entrance: Kleine Budengasse
Daily 10 a.m.–5 p.m.; Closed Mon
»With the elevator into the Roman era«, to the foundation of the Roman praetor's palace of the 1st–4th century, below the city hall.

Rathaus (City Hall)
Tours: Mon, Wed, Sat 3 p.m.
The summerhouse is Cologne's most important Renaissance structure (1569–73), Late Gothic city hall tower, Gothic Hansa hall.

Mikwe
Obenmarspforten/Unter Goldschmied
(next to the historic City Hall)
Mon–Thurs 8 a.m.–5 p.m.,
Fri 8 a.m.–12:30 p.m., Sun 11 a.m. – 1 p.m., keys kept by the doorman of the city hall.
Ritual baths of the oldest Jewish community in Germany.

An Farina
Modern residence- and business area; on the site of the original house of »Farina Gegenüber« the oldest eau de cologne factory. Chronicles of the company: founded in 1709 by Giovanni Marina Farina, in 1714 in began to produce »wonder water«. In 1742 it was called »Eau de Cologne« for the first time, and 20 years later, 1814, the wife of Privy Councillor von Goethe, ordered 16 bottles at one time.

Gülichplatz
Named after Nikolaus Gülich (1644–86) who was decapitated after he had overthrown the city council and tried to rule the city himself. His house on this site was torn down and its reconstruction was forbidden. As a warning, a pillory with his head on it was placed here. It was removed by the French in 1794. Since 1913, it is the site of the **Fastnachtsbrunnen** (Carnival Fountain) by Georg Grasegger.

Gürzenich
Martinstr./Quatermarkt
Daily 10 a.m.–8 p.m.
Traditional place for large festivals, meetings, and since the existence of the philharmonic, for occasional concerts.

St. Maria im Kapitol
(St. Mary in the Capitol)
Marienplatz 19
Daily 9:30 a.m.–6 p.m.

Day 2 – Information

One of the most important sacred buildings in Europe; oldest fur-cated crucifix from Cologne, dated at the beginning of the 14th century. Outside the church and below the apse is the **Lichhof** former cemetery, and the **Dreikönigspförtchen** (Three-Magi Gate), through which, according to legend, the bones of the Holy Three Magi were carried into the city around 1164.

Antoniterkirche
Schildergasse 57
Mon–Fri 11 a.m.–6:20 p.m., Sat 11 a.m.–3 p.m., Sun 9:30 a.m.–7 p.m.
Gothic church of the 14th century. Consecrated in 1384, church of the order of the Anthonians, who were primarily dedicated to the care of the sick. After secularization in 1802, it became the first protestant church of the city. Inside is the »Todesengel« (Angel of Death) by Barlach, 1938, with the features of Käthe Kollwitz. (Second casting. The first casting for the cathedral of Güstrow was destroyed in World War II.)

Käthe Kollwitz Museum of the Kreissparkasse
Neumarkt 18–24
Son–Fri 10 a.m.–5 p.m., Thurs 10 a.m.–8 p.m.
Sketches, sculptures, printed graphics.

St. Aposteln
(Church of the Apostles)
Neumarkt 30
Mon, Wed, Thurs, Fri, Sat 10 a.m.–1 p.m., 2–6 p.m.; Sun 9 a.m.–12:30 p.m.; Closed Tues

One of the more recent Romanesque churches of Cologne, highest Romanesque church tower in Cologne (called »Apostelsklotz«-apostle's block in Cologne slang). It is just over 219 ft. high.

Fassbender
Mittelstr. 12–14 (Entry to the Bazaar de Cologne)
Delicious snacks, and a view of the Apostelnkloster (Cloister of the Apostles).

Brauerei Päffgen
Friesenstr. 64
Daily 10 a.m.–midnight
One of the oldest most respected »cathedrals« of Kölsch beer on tap.

Davidis
Friesenstr. 51
Daily from 12 noon
Bar and restaurant, German-Alsatian cuisine.

Puppenklinik Rust (Doll Clinic)
Friesenstr. 51
»In-patient, out-patient« doll repair; considerable stock of spare parts.

St. Gereon
Gereonsdriesch 2–4
Daily 10 a.m.–noon, 3–5 p.m.
Late Romanesque baptistry, three-aisled crypt with a mosaic floor, 11th century.

Mariensäule
(Mary's Pillar)
Neo Gothic monument by Vincenz Statz, consecrated in 1858, in 1901 transferred from the archiepiscopal palace to the Gereonsdriesch.

Day 2 – Information

Kölnisches Stadtmuseum – Cologne City Museum, 1594–1606

Römerturm (Roman Tower)
Zeughaus-/St.-Apern-Str.
50 A.D. Part of the Roman city wall. Merlons were added around the turn of the century when the Neo Gothic adjacent house was built.

Kölnisches Stadtmuseum
(Cologne City Museum)
Zeughausstr. 1–3, Tel. 221 23 52
Tues–Sun 10 a.m.–5 p.m., Thurs 10 a.m.–8 p.m.; Closed Mon
Tours: Sat 3 p.m., Sun 11 a.m.
Former arsenal (around 1600), and old guardhouse (1840–41). Prussian guardhouse in classicist style, with the history of the city from the 10th century to the present; Documents and objects from the lives of the citizens and from commerce. City archive.

Römerbrunnen
(Roman Fountain)
Designed by Karl Band, 1914/15.

Römermauer (Roman Wall)
1st century A.D. Remains of the wall can be seen among other places, along the Zeughausstr. and also in the south wall of the arsenal itself.

St. Andreas
(Church of St. Andrew)
Komödienstr. 4
(near the cathedral)
Daily 6:30 a.m.–8 p.m.,
Sun till 7 p.m., crypt daily, except Sat, 9:30 a.m.–noon

Alter Wartesaal
(Old Waiting Room)
Hauptbahnhof
Although centrally located, almost an inside tip for an elegant happy hour with excellent drinks during the late afternoon and early evening (also a restaurant). Not to be confused with the disco by the same name next door.

From Roman Roots to Post-Modern Times:
The Inner City of Cologne

The ever windblown plaza in front of the cathedral is once again a meeting and starting point. When it is blowing and swirling here, when the sheets of rain have finally reached the horizontal, then one really learns to appreciate Cologne's churches, museums, and underground Roman labyrinths, because their chambers are weatherpoof.

However, when the sky is friendly, one should perhaps take a moment to look at the inconspicuous **Taubenbrunnen** (Pigeon Fountain) by Ewald Mataré, which has been splashing since 1953. A sculpted *hors d'œuvre* so to speak, compared to the main courses in cultural history which are to follow. The first one is to be found in the **Römisch-Germanischen Museum** (Roman-Germanic Museum).

This institution which, after opening in 1974, was for years one of the most-visited museums in the Federal Republic, owes its preferential spot at the south side of the cathedral to a **Dionysian mosaic** that accidentally came to light during World War II. Today, it is one of the most important pieces of Roman provincial art found on its original site. It has become the heart of the museum and cannot only be seen close up but also from outside through the large windows.

This colorful mosaic, 89.4 square yards in size, whose pictorial motifs relate to the Dionysian cult which can be interpreted in several ways, may once have decorated the dining or ceremony room of a luxurious city villa in the 3rd century A. D.

In general, the modest and unimaginative container-like architecture of the museum, with few exceptions, offers only a limited number of outstanding works of art. However, it has a rich abundance of everyday objects of all sorts, whose effective presentation, done in the manner of department store displays, deliberately avoids all glorification but instead, attempts to convey something of the reality of Roman life.

Tombstone of Poblicius, 1st century A.D. (Roman-Germanic Museum)

By means of themes such as »Agrippa Misses the Land of the Ubier«, »The Military Brings Glass and Ceramics«, »People and Administration in the City«, »Transfer of Goods in the Rhine Harbor«, or »Everyday Pleasures«, each of which is allotted a stone platform, called an »isle«, or a glass showcase, everyday life in the Roman provincial town of Cologne is illustrated. Naturally, art and politics are considered as well as religion and medicine.

Anyone who takes enough time, will find some stimulating items such as perhaps a pair of glass shoes that had been placed in a grave, a glass showcase dedicated to a man, woman, and child, containing beard scissors, mirrors, and wax boards with bronze handles.

Under no circumstances should one be careless enough to omit the **glass collection**, which is of international renown. It contains such rarities like one of the few existing Diatret glasses; or the circus bowl with its surehanded engraving. Likewise, one should not miss the museum's famous **jewelry collection**, whose early medieval collection is a treasure trove of items from the time of migration of nations, which is of world renown.

After visiting the museum, which for many experts embodies the prototype of archeological museums, the Roman theme is briefly interrupted, until at the end of the tour, past the Köselsche bookstore in the Diocesan Museum, and the historic Brauhaus (brewery) Sion, it is again found in the form of the Roman **Praetorium** under the present city hall.

Here, where history can be precisely traced layer by layer, Cologne's pride in its long and glorious past is immediately sensed. At first, the Praetorium was the official seat of the commander-in-chief of the lower Germanic army. Then it became the service and administration building of the viceroy of the province of Lower Germania, and since the 3rd century A.D., the occasional residence of Roman imperators. After the withdrawal of the Romans, Merovingian kings resided here.

Even if a visitor less versed in archeology sees the exposed foundations, he can hardly get an accurate idea of the former shape of the extensive, often rebuilt and repeatedly altered buildings. He will still be awed by the impressiveness of the building with its outstanding octagon, rising high in its center, whose imperial splendor still speaks to us from the ruins. Although an exact model of the most recent arrangement of the building does not quite correspond with the latest research data, it still effectively assists the somewhat overtaxed imagination of the viewer.

Hardly less interlocking than its ancient predecessor is the Cologne **city hall**, which consists of several buildings erected in the course of centuries. It, too, can look back at a long history because it was first mentioned in the early 12th century.

It is dominated by a tower built in the style of a Flemish belfry by the guilds as a sign of municipal independence after the patrician government of the city was deposed.

The **city hall tower**, 200 feet high, after suffering very heavy damage during the war, is now being restored. Together with the cathedral and Gross St. Martin it represents as before the traditional Rhine panorama. Presently, efforts are being made to place statues of important figures from Cologne's history on pedestals. A serious problem has come up: the medieval program failed to establish a quota for statue selection of historically important women of Cologne. They must find some plausible figures.

If, in this way, the Late Gothic tower attempts to achieve a feministic imprint, the **Renaissance arcade**, from whose balcony decisions by the council were proclaimed, at a closer look reveals itself as being unequivocally masculine: the relief on the central parapet plate portrays the heroic battle between the legendary mayor Grin and a lion, which is interpreted as a parable of the city's battle for independence.

Within the interior of the city hall, to a large extent constructed during the post-war period, there is the attractive **Löwenhof** (Lion Courtyard), surrounded by two-story arcades. Also, there are the splendid tracery and Late Gothic wooden figures of the Nine Good Heroes as well as eight figures of prophets, originally installed in the »Prophetenkammer« (Prophets' Chamber), which decorate the **Hansasaal** (Hansa Hall), that are worth a visit.

The open space in front of the city hall, above and below ground, proves to be a gold mine of background settings of the city's history. The remains of the palace auditorium of the Praetorium, residence of the Roman viceroy, are plainly visible, as well as those of the recently restored 12th century **Mikwe**, the Jewish ritual bath. It is evident that this was once the center of the Jewish quarter. And anyone standing with his back to the city hall and the Roman excavations may by carefully examining the ground, discover the outlines of the old council chapel marked by darker stones laid there.

Opposite the former ancestral home of the fragrant water firm, **Farina**, now in new splendor and with a new function, stands an elegant complex of luxury apartments, stores, and an inner courtyard open to the public. It is flanked by a »rain-proof« arcade with stores, a café, and an ingenious fountain created by Anneliese Langenbach, where »The Woman in Changing Times« figuratively passes in review. Those who wish to enjoy a view of the city while splashing in a bath tub high above the city, must move into one of the penthouses of »An Farina« quarter.

Across from it at the »House Neuerburg«, on a spot named after the freedom fighter Nikolaus Gülich, stands the unusual **Fastnachtsbrunnen** (Carnival Fountain) whose bronze cheeks, next to the dancing figures of »*hillige Knechte und Mägde*« (man-servants and maids), are gathered about the much recited

Renaissance Arcade of the City Hall, 1569–73, by Wilhelm Vernukken

verse which Johann Wolfgang von Goethe, German writer and one of the giants of world literature, sent in reply to an invitation to the carnival celebration:

> *Löblich wird ein tolles Streben,*
> *Wenn es kurz ist und mit Sinn,*
> *Heiterkeit zum Erdenleben*
> *Sei dem flücht'gen Rausch Gewinn.*

(Laudible becomes a driving ambition, When it is short-lived and with reason, Joy in life on earth, Will be the result of the fleeting delirium.)

The **Gürzenich**, known outside Cologne probably because of the orchestra by the same name, or possibly because of the carnival meetings which are televised from here, derived its name from the patrician family Gürzenich. Their name was also given to the

2 impressive dance and festival hall which was erected on their property in 1437, and was supposed to surpass comparable buildings in other cities.

The ponderous exterior with octagonal corner towers, perforated by high narrow windows, and a pewter parapet covered by finely crafted tracery, epitomizes Cologne's civic houses of the 15th century, whose design had become increasingly more grandiose. The banquet hall on the upper floor was splendidly decorated with wall tapestries and other ornaments. Here, mayors dined, banquets were given, and festivities held. Also kings and emperors were received here. When later it was reduced to use as a warehouse, the banquet hall was changed and enlarged during the last century.

After the destruction of World War II, Karl Band and Rudolf Schwarz rebuilt part of the Gürzenich. They created a new architecture, including Cologne's most elegant **flight of stairs**, an example of the architecture of the 50s which is becoming of late more and more appreciated.

This flight of stairs connects the Gürzenich with the former **St. Alban church** whose ruins were made a »memorial for the destruction and the dead of world wars«, a conscious and effective contrast to the festiveness of the Gürzenich. A copy of the kneeling figures of the »**Trauerndes Elternpaar**« (Grieving Parents), by Käthe Kollwitz, bestows a quiet urgency upon this visible reminder, from which one cannot escape. One should also defintely go up the handsome flight of stairs and walk along the separating yet unifying brick wall.

From the corner of Gürzenichstrasse, one passes through the Kleine Sandkaul into the heavily travelled Augustiner and Pipinstrasse respectively. Rather abruptly, the walk returns to the every day life of Cologne: a turning point between the architectural past and present, between aesthetic vanishing points of the Gürzenich and that church which many consider the most impressive Romanesque church in Cologne — St. Maria im Kapitol (St. Mary in the Capitol). Without question, a walk through time and space has its cut-off points and faults, sharp corners and edges, which after all comprise the architectural conglomerate of a metropolis.

Now we come close to the mighty building above the tranquil **Lichhof** (once burial ground), cast a glance at the sculpture of the »Mourners«, created in 1946—49 by Gerhard Marcks; descend through the picturesque »**Dreikönigspförtchen**« (Three-Magi Gate) to the Marienplatz, and keeping to the right, continue to the Kasinostrasse — almost a circular tour.

The New Flight of Stairs of the Gürzenich, by Rudolf Schwarz and Karl Band, 1952–55

Across from the entrance one reads a sign on the welfare home, where shortly before the stores close some rather desolate young people with bulging plastic bags are heading for the former abbess home of the St. Maria im Kapitol convent. It has seen more romantic days, especially between 1804 and 1806, when Friedrich Schlegel lived here.

Cologne's frequent reference to its Roman past greets us also in **St. Maria im Kapitol** (St. Mary in the Capitol), a surname »in Capitolio« that unequivocally refers to the Roman capitol, was documented only in the 12th century, but is based on archeologically proven facts. The former convent church was built in the

11th century on the foundations of a temple dedicated to the Capitoline gods Jupiter, Juno, and Minerva. Even more, the width of the church's aisles was determined by the dimensions of the Roman temple.

In many respects, the highy complex architecture, rightly considered as »the brainchild of the Rhenish Romanesque«, is an example of the transmission of meanings by seizing upon certain architectural forms. The cloverleaf or three-conch ground plans obviously follow the model of the church of the Nativity in Bethlehem, and thereby demonstrate that this church is dedicated to the mother of God. The archbishop of Cologne traditionally celebrated the first Christmas mass before the cathedral.

On the – literally and figuratively – other side, the design of the **interior wall of the western aisle** precisely duplicates the interior of the Aix-la-Chapelle Palatine chapel. It is not by chance that the

Church of St. Maria im Kapitol (Mary in the Capitol): wooden door (detail). Offering in the Temple, and Baptism in the Jordan, before 1065

wall has imperial overtones because the woman who built it, Abbess Ida, descended from the imperial line of the Ottonians. Although their reign had already come to an end, their female descendant felt that she had to call upon architecture as a reminder of their past greatness. The recently restored interior is highly impressive because of its spaciousness despite the fact that the view into the choir is interrupted by the **Renaissance choir screen** made in Mecheln. Its obviously over-sized width was

Church of St. Maria im Kapitol (Mary in the Capitol): view to the north from the south conch

perhaps caused by the fact that the difference between Cologne and Mecheln measurement units was not taken into consideration at the time the order was placed. If the wooden ceiling installed in the 50s above the weighty pillar arcades of the nave appears today to be somewhat tasteless, one should consider that the Gothic arched ceiling which was destroyed during the war, (traces are still on the walls) corresponded even less to the flat-roof of the original.

Shopper's Paradise in Cinemascope format: Hohe Strasse…

There may be divided opinions about the nave – the gigantic **three-conch choir** – behind the choir screen which is sometimes used for concerts because of its outstanding acoustics. But, it is one of the most impressively spacious creations of the Romanesque period. No less impressive is the crypt with its mighty cubiforms surpassed only by those of the Speyer Cathedral.

Also of note are the remaining furnishings, especially the **wooden doors** of the former entrance at the north conch now installed at the south side aisle. They are a unique treasure. The history of art does not know of anything comparable to the wooden relief from the middle of the 11th century, at one time colorfully painted which depicts with sparkling originality, the story of Christ.

Outside in front of the church, another abrupt change of attractions and themes, symptomatic of Cologne, begins. More than in any other large cities of Europe due to vast wartime destruction, the salvaged structural treasures of Cologne are like islands scattered in an ocean of modern, mostly monotonous, buildings. They cannot be viewed as structural ensembles nor are they even homogeneous with respect to the city. This means that tours of art and history are rarely continuous but proceed from point to point among municipal wastelands – in short, a kind of leap frogging.

… and Schildergasse (taken with a 360 degree camera)

In this instance, the leap lands beyond the Pipinstrasse at the classicistic façade of the **Kaufhof** (department store), 1912–14, and further on at the **Hohe Strasse** and **Schildergasse**, Cologne's shopping center. As early as 1965, this pair of streets had already been revamped to become the first pedestrian zone in the Federal Republic; then, it was a model of car-free shopping streets – today it is commonplace.

Halfway down the Schildergasse, the **Antoniter church** provides 10-minute services, pauses for meditation in the rat-race of shopping. Especially worth seeing in the little Gothic church is Ernst Barlach's sculpture »**Angel of Death**« suspended by a chain.

Passing by the store windows of the »Bücherstube« (bookstore) on the right side of the Zeppelinstrasse, one arrives at the contemporary nonplusultra of Cologne industrial arcitecture, the **Olivandenhof**. At first, its exterior design appears to be conservative. The 1913 façade, which is rated as a national monument, was cleared of rubble and completely restored, using the then typical natural stone materials, tuff and basalt lava. However, inside modern tungsten steel- and glass architecture, which has since become familiar from Dallas to Stuttgart, from Toronto to Hamburg, is predominant. The 8,900 square yards of sales space on four floors offer a marvelous diversity of items.

The bright inner court is domed by an oval glass cupola, and is traversed by glassed escalators and glass elevators – an innovative municipal construction which recently was awarded a prize as »European Shopping Center of the Year» by a jury of international experts.

Olivandenhof? »*Olvund*« and »*Ollivand*« are medieval terms for elephant. And »Zum Olfunden« was a cloister which stood here about 1268. Later, it became the cloister and church »Santa Maria ad Olivas«. At the beginning of our century, it then became a commercial establishment carrying its present name.

After walking through this shopping paradise, the tour continues over Richmodstrasse to the Neumarkt, past an old established Cologne curiosity – »Gummi Grün«, a speciality store whose items are all made of a natural elastic product. If you don't believe it, walk in. You can trust your eyes and especially your nose.

On the opposite side, a tower with horse heads recalls an old Cologne saga. During the 14th century, a newly-wed patrician lady Richmodis died during a plague epidemic and was buried in the nearby cemetery of St. Aposteln. During the night, grave rob-

Sidewalk Café in front of the Antoniterkirche on the Schildergasse

Olivandenhof (1978/88). Architects: Hentrich, Petschnigg, and Partner)

bers opened the coffin. Suddenly the lady, presumed dead, rose up, staggered to her house and knocked at the door. The grieving husband did not believe his eyes and he allegedly said, »My two horses will sooner run up the stairs than my wife be standing alive in front of the door.« Just at that moment, the hooves of horses could be heard on the steps and his two white horses were seen looking out of the tower. The Richmodishaus also offers something of note: the composer Max Bruch was born here, (»Ah, the one with the violin concert...«), best known composer native to Cologne besides Jacques Offenbach.

At the end of the street appears the **Neumarkt** (New Market). Despite its central location, this open, clear space is rather isolated from the circulating traffic, and its lack of style cannot be altered even by the attractive choir section of St. Aposteln.

Stairway Tower of the Richmodishaus at the Neumarkt

In some respects however, the Neumarkt has remained true to its tradition. Recently it has become a new market for books. There, where troops once marched, and where today, during public events droves of people gather, the North Rhine-Westphalien book wholesalers have their gathering.

Below ground, the Neumarkt may also soon create a sensation because Cologne archeologists are eager to know if there are Roman artifacts there. They surmise that there may be something slumbering which may be unique in Europe.

On the right, a few yards towards the **Neumarkt Passage** is the building complex of the district savings bank. It has a most appealing interior, created by the choice of building materials, coloring, and lighting. (Built in 1988.) Sandstone, highly polished pink marble offsetting the green painted I-beams and granite

Neumarkt with Eye-catcher: St. Aposteln

floors add an unusual flavor to the building. Literature (in the Buchhaus »Gonski« – Gonski's bookstore), culinary and vegetarian delicacies compete for attention in and between both patios. In the rear, octagonal court, one can float in a glass space glider toward the **Käthe Kollwitz Museum.**

From here it is only a few steps to the side entrance of **St. Aposteln** (Church of the Apostles). How effective the solution of the design of St. Maria im Kapitol had been for the development of the Rhenish Romanic, is impressively shown by the three-conch choir of St. Aposteln which was created a century later, an exceedingly rich, well articulated central building, seemingly at peace with itself.

Accentuated by two octagonal stairway towers covered by pleated domes between the conches, and a lantern-crowned

View of the Gerling Corporation building at the Gereonshof

square tower, the east layout of St. Aposteln not only conveys a lasting impression of the rich form of the Rhenish Romanic, but also of the medieval concept of the city of heaven. It was believed to be represented concretely by such architecture. In counterbalance to the cloverleaf choir facing the city, the high tower in front of the mighty transept draws the eye of those who approach it from the west. At the time of its erection, it was still outside the early medieval city walls.

The interior of the nave, whose renovation has raised mixed emotions, reveals, upon careful exam, changes in the original Salian structure. In the square cupola, after the loss of the 19th century mosaic to the war, a daring and thoroughly appealing attempt was made, not to imitate something of the effect of the original colors, but to have a creative empathy.

The area in front of the church which also hosts the few weekly markets of the inner city is an example of the recent efforts concerning the care of monuments. After restoring Romanesque churches, they will also improve their surroundings and create mini parks – primarily through interesting pavements, landscaping, and unrelenting safeguards against illegally parked cars.

Opposite the west side of the church, one should take a glance at the »**Bazaar de Cologne**«: a roofed, two-story shopping center (1980/81) with many snack bars in a relatively small space, a small-scaled *galleria coloniensis*.

Across the so-called »**Boulevard Mittelstrasse**«, whose title, with other street trappings, is an attempt to legitimize the products offered and prices charged by the elegant stores, the route leads through the no less immodest **Pfeilstrasse**. It tries to refute the canard that one has to drive to Düsseldorf for shopping. At the end of the short street, to the right and left, is the **Ehrenstrasse** where prices are still a little less advanced. Its gaudy boutiques are at present geared to the fashionable teenager and young adult culture made obvious by the loudness of disco music. Its obviously lucrative clothing scene has long ago cooked the goose of many of the originial establishments: seafood restaurants, cafés, and pancake stalls.

On the other hand, the more appealing **Friesenwall** has undergone an astonishing change. Its little restaurants and antique stores already are an indication that the **Friesenstrasse** is a model for revitalizing and cleaning up the old city. Here, in the immediate neighborhood of the Gerling Insurance Corporation, new houses and hotels have been built which often substantially adhere to the old structural motifs.

Architectural recycling appears to be a typical Cologne activity. In many instances, at the beginning of new projects in the inner city, historic façades remain standing like the illusory Potemkin villages, until as a matter of course, they were included in the reconstruction. In this manner, thanks to the vehement actions of Cologne's conservator Hiltrud Kier, many segments of buildings worth keeping were saved from the pick axe.

Doll Clinic in the Friesenstrasse

The tidying-up of the Friesenstrasse however has definitely left its characteristic Cologne lifestyle enough air to breathe. The foremost example is the »Brauhaus (brewery) Päffgen«, one of those »cathedrals« of Kölsch beer – always good for a hearty refreshment. A treat for lovers of curiosities is at the Spiesergasse in the form of the »Puppenklinik« (Doll Clinic). A tiny shop, it brings damaged dolls back to health through surgery and the implanting of substitute parts. The stock of saucer-like eyes, tiny pink arms and legs and hair styles is indeed worth seeing.

Through the Spiesergasse, past the Gerling Corporation one arrives at the Gereonskloster, a quiet and quieting oasis, surrounded by attractively diversified architecture and dominated by the mighty decagon of **St. Gereon**.

Along with the cathedral, this church had always been regarded as the highest ranking of the Cologne archdiocese, as well as the most noble Cologne religious establishment up until the secularization under French rule at the beginning of the 19th century, when all were dissolved.

The core of today's church is a late antique oval building whose age is made apparent by the types of building materials used. Although refuted archeologically, it dates back to the legend of Helena, mother of Emperor Constantine, who supposedly erected a church above the graves of the Holy Gereon, one of Cologne's city patrons, and other martyrs. What is certain, however, is that Archbishop Anno, one of the most energetic builders in medieval Cologne, did order the construction of the existing nave and its crypt below in the 11th century. Barely a century later, it was lengthened and furnished with a new apse and two striking flanking towers. During the early 13th century, the oval building from the 4th century was finally changed to a domed **decagon** which for medieval architecture, is not unique only to Cologne.

Looking up at the dome, the most significant since the Hagia Sophia in Constantinople and the Florentine dome by Brunelleschi, is a breathtaking architectural experience. The splendor of the lavishly rich walls of the four floors rising one above the other is heightened by the glowing red of the recently re-painted cupola which, like the golden flames, alludes to the fact that this church stands above the graves of martyrs. While the new glass windows, created by Georg Meistermann, blend in congenially – as do most buildings of historic Cologne which were severely damaged during the war – with the inherited creative process of medieval architecture. However, the placing of a Baroque high altar salvaged from another church is not without problems because it

Church of St. Gereon: Ceiling Vault of the Decagon

blocks the view of the central area, and almost overwhelms the choir aisle, and in addition, also suggests an apparent historical continuity which has never existed in this present form.

In front of the east side of the church, the Gereonsdriesch plaza keeps the noise and hectic activities of the Christophstrasse at a distance. The Mariensäule (Mary's Pillar) as well as the linden trees planted by Joseph Beuys in 1985, are well-suited to the serenity of the plaza.

Taking the Steinfeldergasse back toward the Magnusstrasse, one finds the **Römerturm** (Roman Tower). Allegedly its fate as the best preserved monument of the Roman city wall of Cologne is owed to the circumstance that, during the Middle Ages, it was used as a latrine! This former north-west tower of Roman Cologne, which was elevated to city status in 50 A. D., is remarkable. Its almost square shape, which was surrounded by a wall about 2.5 miles long, that was partitioned by 19 towers, is noteworthy, not only because of its excellent state of preservation, but because of its ornamentation: circles, rhombs, and little temple façades incorporated into its brickwork as bright stone mosaics. (Friends of both old and new art may at this point decide to take a detour to the galleries and art shops on St.-Apern-Strasse and the Kreishausgalerie. They can then rejoin the general route by walking through Helenenstrasse and the idyllic children's playground at the Römerturm.)

From the Römerturm, the partially preserved **Roman city wall** leads east to the cathedral, joins the brickwork of the city museum on the south side, and then runs into the **Römerbrunnen** (Roman Fountain). It was erected in 1915 and reconstructed in simplified form after World War II, to keep alive the memory of the founding of this city by Romans, and whose construction is based upon the foundation plan of another tower of the Roman wall.

The Zeughaus (Arsenal), erected at the turn of the 17th century, is an elongated brick structure with stepped gables, whose appearance today is accentuated by the city colors of Cologne, red and white, painted on the shutters. It once housed Cologne's arsenal, but it is now the home of the **Stadtmuseum** (Cologne City Museum) which attempts to present Cologne's history in all its facets, from the Middle Ages to the most recent era. It does not exclude the time of the »Tausendjährigen Reiches« (Thousand-Year-Reich), an era commonly stricken from memory.

Naturally, one can have different opinions of some presentations which at times are somewhat simple in their attempts to draw upon accidentally preserved historical objects, as well as to portray their relevant culture. However, one should consider that it is always easier to present a few surviving pieces of art, whose effectiveness, because of their aesthetic quality, has lasted beyond their original periods, than to portray them as history, which occurs only once and remains tangible only in its relics or results, which in turn are history themselves.

Nevertheless, anyone interested in history, will get his money's worth in the city museum. Also, a person who is more impressed by visible phenomena rather than historical roots, will be enthused by the large city model, created in accordance with Arnold

Römerturm (Roman Tower)

Mercator's plan of the city of 1571. This first bird's eye view of Cologne, which by means of a lighting program, and an elucidation in Cologne colloquialism, worthwhile hearing, will also highlight the optical experience accustically. Moreover, anyone who has overlooked it as he entered, should, when leaving, cast a glance at a little glass showcase directly at the entrance. Therein, a remarkable attempt, which was doomed to failure from the onset, is made to portray the *»Kölschen Klüngel«* (Cologne coterie), which purports to show the lifestyle of Cologne at all levels – an impossibility.

From the exposed remains of the Roman wall at the intersection of Komödienstrasse and the Nord-Süd Fahrt (north-south drive), stairs lead up the castle wall to a quiet alley. On the right lies the estate of the cathedral community, meaning its gates, behind which the clerical garden paradise is more hidden than visible — a green idyl one does not expect to find in the middle of the city, and whose total proportions can only be observed from the cathedral tower.

The tranquil castle wall forms an axis with the west side of the cathedral and constantly lures tourists into the fruitless attempt to view the full front of the cathedral by walking backwards while at the same time craning their necks upwards.

At about the halfway point, a staircase on the left provides a clear view of **St. Andreas** (Church of St. Andrew). Its two-story, octagonal tower, with its typical pleated roof above the trigon gables, creates a remarkable Romanesque accent among the domineering impact of the Gothic cathedral towers, the rather uninspired masses of post-war buildings, which spread west from the cathedral along the former Roman city wall.

How rich the Romanesque architecture can be is not only shown by the splendid friezes, blind arcades, and chapiters above the thickset supports that decorate the nave of the Stauffer era, which, beyond the dim, squarish cupola, dramatically opens into the light-swept glassed hall of the Late Gothic aisle. The vestibule of the mighty west building which, with its dentalated encircling arches, gives it an exotic appearance.

In the crypt of the former monastery, now the Dominican church, rest the bones of the learned Dominican saint Albertus Magnus who, like nobody else, shaped the thinking of the Middle Ages.

Over the Komödienstrasse, past the »Buchhandlung Herder« (Herder bookstore), and the municipal tourist office we again approach today's starting point: the cathedral.

Day 3 – Program: South Side of Town – Rings – St. Pantaleon – Aachener Weiher – Rings – Eigelstein – Cathedral – Oper – St. Kolumba – Hohe Strasse – Cathedral Square

Morning	St. Severin (Parking) – Severinstor – Sachsenring – Ulrepforte – City Wall – St. Pantaleon (Parking) – Ring – Barbarossaplatz – Roonstrasse – Lindenstrasse – Kanalstrasse – Ostasiatisches Museum
Noon	Short stop at the Aachener Pond – Restaurant in the Ostasiatische Museum – Japanisches Kulturinstitut
Afternoon	Rudolfplatz – Rings – Ebertplatz – Eigelstein – Parking Garage of the Cathedral – Museum für Angewandte Kunst – Minoritenkirche – Opernhaus – 4711 – WDR – Dischhaus – St. Kolumba – Hohe Strasse – Stollwerck-Passage
Afterwards	Dom-Hotel-Terrassen: Farewell to Cologne

> **For users of public transportation (KVB):**
> **Cathedral – Clodwigplatz:** Bus line 132 (Meschenich) 6 stops;
> **Clodwigplatz – Eifelstrasse:** Streetcar line 6 (Longerich), line 15 (Thielenbruch), line 16 (Mülheim), 2 stops;
> **Eifelstrasse – Rudolfplatz:** Streetcar line 6 (Longerich), line 10 (Merkenich), line 15 (Thielenbruch), 3 stops;
> **Rudolfplatz – Kanalstrasse:** Streetcar line 1 (Junkersdorf), line 2 (Frechen), 2 stops;
> **Kanalstrasse – Neumarkt – Cathedral:** Streetcar line 1 (Bensberg), line 2 (Ostheim), 3 stops;
> At Neumarkt, change to subway:
> Streetcar line 9 (Chorweiler), line 12 (Merkenich, line 14 (Dom/Hbf.-Cathedral/Main Train Station), line 16 (Mülheim), 2 stops.
> Since the subway is underground, one cannot see everything described here.

Day 3 – Information

St. Severin
(Church of St. Severin)
Im Ferkulum 29
Daily 8:30 a.m.–noon,
3–7 p.m., Sun 9 a.m.–noon
Former collegiate church of the 11th/13th centuries. Crypt with wall paintings of the 14th century. Guided tour and visit to the Roman-Franconian cemeteries Fri 4:30 p.m.

Haus Balchem
Severinstr. 15
Large Baroque mansion of 1676. It was originally named »Zum Goldenen Bären« (Golden Bear). The name Balchem goes back to the owners at the turn of the century, the Balchem Brothers beer brewers. Today it is a municipal library.

Früh em Veedel
Chlodwigplatz 28
11 a.m.–1 p.m., exept Sun
A Cologne inn rich in tradition.

Severinstorburg
Chlodwigplatz
One of the three preserved medieval city gates, dating back to the 12th/13th centuries.

Chlodwigplatz/Salierring
Named after the Franconian King Chlodwig I, (about 466–511). Around 508, he incorporated the Rhine-Franconian royal palatinate and realm of his relative King Sigibert into his kingdom.

Ulrepforte/City Wall
(Sachsenring)
Remains of the medieval city wall with two towers, city gate, which was later walled up. In the wall, the oldest secular monument of Germany (»Ulredenkmal«, 1360).

St. Pantaleon
(Church of St. Pantaleon)
Am Pantaleonsberg 2
Mon–Sun 8:15 a.m.–5 p.m.
Former cloister church of the

Day 3 – Information

Benedictines. Oldest Romanesque church of Cologne, erected in the 10th century. The former sanctuary of the cloister is the only one in Cologne.

Rudolfplatz

In the center of this reconstructed square is the Hahnentor, a ponderours twin towered gate of the 13th century. This is the spot where during the Middle Ages, German kings, returning from the coronation in Aix-la-Chapelle, entered the city in order to worship the relics of the Holy Three Magi.

Museum für Ostasiatische Kunst

(Museum of East-Asian Art)
Universitätsstr. 100
Tel. 405038
Tues–Sun 10 a.m.–5 p.m., first Fri of the month 10 a.m.–8 p.m.; Closed Mon; Tours: Sun 11 a.m.
New construction of the museum 1977. Oldest European museum of East-Asian art exclusively since 1913. Most extensive East Asian art collection of the Federal Republic of Germany.

Cafeteria

(Hours are the same at those of the museum)
View of the Aachener pond from the 20s, created as a modern recreation facility during the construction of the green belt.

Japanisches Kulturinstitut

(Japanese Culture Institute)
Universitätsstr. 98
Public non-lending library (15,000 books)
Mon 2–5 p.m., Tues–Fri 9 a.m.–1 p.m., 2–5 p.m.

Rings

Attractive promenade dating from the end of the 19th century. It runs in a semi-circle around the inner city. It was built on the levelled moat of the medieval city wall which was demolished in 1881. A generously-designed boulevard, fashioned after Parisian and Viennese models, with parkways, fountains, and monuments. Reconstructed since the completion of the Ring subway. Especially seen in the Kaiser-Wilhelm-Ring area.

Stadtmauer (City Wall)

Hansaring/Am Kümpchenshof/Gereonswall
Remains of the medieval city wall with the Gereon mill tower of the 14th century. Now used as a residence.

Hansa-Gymnasium

(High School)
Hansaring 54–58
Former commercial college, erected in 1898/99. Architect: F. C. Heimanns, opened in 1901, transfered to the Rhine bank in 1907, today a municipal high school.

Hansa-Hochhaus (Skyscraper)

Hansaring 97
1924/25, architect Jakob Koerfer. 17 floors (214.5 ft.). At the time of its construction, the highest skyscraper in Europe; today, office of the Saturn Co.

Ebertplatz

Hexagonal skyscraper »Gerlings Bleistift« (Gerling's Pencil),

Day 3 – Information

»Water Kinetic Plastic« by Wolfgang Göddertz, 1977.

Eigelsteintorburg

Medieval city gate, 13th century, with a sculpture of the *»Kölsche Boor«* (boy; 19th century). In the medieval hierachy of German cities, Cologne was classed with status of the farmers. The farmer still exists today as one of the figures of the triumvirate during Cologne's carnival.

St. Mariä Himmelfahrt

(Church of the Assumption of the Blessed Virgin)
Marzellenstr. 32–40
(near Cathedral)
Mon–Wed 7:45 a.m.–noon, 12:45–4:30 p.m., Thurs–Fri 12:45–4:30 p.m.
Former Jesuit church early 17th century. The order's most important building in north-west Germany. Concerts are frequently held here.

Museum für Angewandte Kunst

(Museum of Applied Arts)
An der Rechtschule
Tel. 22 12 9 95
Tues 10 a.m.–8 p.m., Wed–Sun 10 a.m.–5 p.m.; Closed Mon
Tours: Sun 11:30 a.m., Tues 6:30 p.m.
One of the four internationally important collections of its kind in the Federal Republic of Germany. The museum houses over 100,000 works of art. From a precious small piece of jewelry to complete room furnishing, it continuously presents outstanding evidence of European life and living over 1,000 years and of all areas of handicraft as well as modern designs. Parallel to it is the graphics department with about 70,000 prints of almost all kinds of applied graphics from the 16th century to today.

Boisserée

Art store and gallery
Drususgasse 7–11
(near Museum of Applied Arts)
Tel. 21 45 74
Opened 150 years ago by two nephews of the famous art historians and collectors Sulpiz and Melchior Boisserée who successfully worked for the completion of the cathedral. Art of the 20th century, bronzes, modern glass.

Minoritenkirche

(Minoriten Church)
Kolpingplatz
Daily from 7:30 a.m.–6:30 p.m.
The only church in Cologne of an order dedicated to a life of poverty. It belonged to the Franciscans, also called »Minorite Brothers« (Minoriten in Latin). Building from the 13th/14th century, Late Gothic transept, preserved in a few arches (integrated into the inner court of the Museum of Applied Arts). Graves of the Franciscan pater and theologian Johannes Duns Scotus who died in 1308, and the fellow pater and founder of the Kolping works, Adolf Kolping (1813–65), sculpture of Adolf Kolping, 1903, by J. B. Schreiner in front of the west façade.

Oper (Opera)
Offenbachplatz

Day 3 – Information

1954–57. 1,346 seats, in the court of the opera fountain by Hans Jürgen Grümmer, 1966.

4711
Glockengasse/Schwertnergasse
Ancestral house of the 4711 company. Reconstructed after the war, duplicating the 1852–54 Neo Gothic building.

WDR
Appellhofplatz 1
Largest state radio establishment in Europe. 4 radio programs with about 111 broadcasting hours, and one regional television program. 4,500 employees.

Dischhaus
Brückenstr./Herzogstr.
Built in 1929 by architect Bruno Paul. An elegant, stream lined office and business building from the late 20s. Extensively renovated in 1983/84. It has a staircase that is worth seeing.

St. Kolumba
(Church of St. Kolumba)
Kolumbastr. 2
Daily 6:30 a.m.–7 p.m.
The so-called »Madonna in the Ruins«, former parish church of the 13th/15th centuries, was completely destroyed during the war except the outer walls. In 1950, the present chapel was built among the ruins of the old church in honor of the Mary statue which miracuously survived. Architect Gottfried Böhm. Tabernacle altar made of marble by Elisabeth Treskow. Wooden figure of the Holy Antonius by Ewald Mataré, 1937. West window by Georg Meistermann, 1948.

Sauer
Minoritenstr. 13
(near Minoriten Church)
A company, rich in tradition, for lady's and gentlemen's fashions. Founded in 1842. Since 1986, in a new building with Post-Modern elegance.

Hohe Strasse
One of Cologne's main streets for shopping. Even during the time of the Romans it ran in this direction. Then, it was the main connection between the southern and the northern city gates of the Roman settlement. 100,000 people crowd it daily.

Café Eigel
Brückenstr. 1–3 (near Hohe Str.)
Mon–Fri 9 a.m.–7 p.m., Sat 9 a.m.–6 p.m., Sun 2–6 p.m.
Elegant ambience for coffee and cake.

Stollwerck-Passage
Roofed connection between Hohe Strasse and Am Hof. Only remaining shopping arcade from the turn of the century (1907) at the then still elegant Hohe Strasse.

Dom-Hotel-Terrassen
May: daily 11 a.m.–5:30 p.m., June–Oct.: daily 11 a.m.–11 p.m.

Cologne in a Semi-Circle:
South Side of Town – Rings – Eigelstein

»*Fresh water, fresh courage!*«
(Graffiti at the Academy of Art
and Design, Maternusstrasse)

All good things come in threes: ergo, the last day should round off our knowledge of Cologne, but this time not on foot, but by car, public transportation, or by taxi.

Although this route does not form a complete circle, it does make a semi-circle along the ring streets. It also contains a special Cologne encore, a brief visit to a quarter or »*Veedel*« as the suburb south of the city is called.

Strictly speaking, it is not a real suburb like Sülz, Ehrenfeld, or Nippes. Still, among the 84 districts that comprise Cologne's population of almost one million, it is without question one of the most unusual city quarters. Indeed, it has for years regarded itself as the quarter par excellence – or so regarded by others.

Self-esteem and image, reality and myth, can hardly be separated around the Chlodwigplatz. However, for a brief visit on an ordinary morning, this is not necessary.

View of the Church of St. Severin through the Severinsmühlengasse

Cologne Girl in the Severin quarter

Traditional Cologne pub: »Früh em Veedel« which is nicknamed »Invalidendom«, Chlodwigplatz ▶

From the cathedral, it is best to drive by car along the Rhine bank, through the Rhine tunnel, under the elegant pylon-crowned Severinsbrücke (bridge), past the pink-tinted church St. Maria Lyskirchen, and the old harbor docks. Shortly before the so-called »Siebengebirge« (Seven Hills), the distinctive warehouses of the Agrippina wharf (1908/09, by Hans Verbeek) the Ubierring turns to the right.

The Rautenstrauch-Joest-Museum houses the ethnological collection, and further ahead on the opposite side in the Cologne Academy of Art and Design is the home of students and professors of aesthetic education – a clientel that provides a certain Bohemian atmosphere to this district.

At the **Bottmühle** (mill), one drives on the right toward its completely green tower. This pretty eyecatcher once belonged to a mill in the city wall; today the red flag of the »Falcons« waves from its top.

The little street ends at the new dwellings on the former »**Stollwerckgelände**« (former industrial plant of the Stollwerck AG). When in the early 80s the demolition of the factory was threatened, bitter opposition raged there and throughout West Germany. Gone was the sweet chocolate aroma which, alternating with the vapor of the hops of the breweries, was for a long time the typical mélange of scent here.

Meanwhile the battle with the house squatters has come to an end. Only a part of the factory escaped demolition but nevertheless a remarkable community was built on its grounds. It has approximately 1,400 tenants in over 800 dwellings, almost exclusively low-cost housing. The occupants of a home for old people, Turkish children, and »*kölsche Pänz*« live in harmony in the inner court. (The number of foreigners is presently less than 30 percent.) True, the grass could be a few years older, the vegetation greener, the idle land along the Annostrasse fixed up, but it is far from being an »asylum for gnomes« or a »ready-made idyll« as the local press initially described it.

From Annostrasse, the Severinsmühlengasse leads directly to the slender choir of the church of **St. Serverin**. Like most of the large churches in Cologne, it too rises above a cemetery from the Roman times. The Holy Severin, Cologne's third bishop, has his grave site here. In the present structure of the church, which dates back to the 4th century, one can discern almost every phase of Cologne's medieval architecture from the Late Romanesque choir to the domineering west tower covered by Late Gothic tracery, which was not completed until the 16th century. Together, with the sharp-edged flanks of the choir towers, it accents the southern Cologne Rhine panorama.

The interior of the choir is impressive. Its original furnishings are quite well preserved, beginning with the precious mosaic floor of white, pink, and black marble; the two rows of choir pews with fancifully carved animals; and the remarkable structure behind the altar, whose four Romanesque pillars now support the Neo Gothic Severin shrine. Thus, the shrine could not only be seen from a distance, but one could also pass under it to experience the holy aura which supposedly emanates from the relics preserved in the shrine. Behind it is a precious piece of Romanesque architecture – the vault of the Aegidius choir with its suspended keystone.

Lastly, attention should be invited to another feature which demonstrates how classic architectural theory was applied during the Middle Ages. The trumpets of the angels in the corner of the murals above the choir pews, end in sound-holes behind which stoneware pots are set into the walls. Vitruv, author of the only architectural treatise handed down from the Graeco-Roman era, had recommended a similar idea for the construction of theaters in order to improve acoustics.

The **Severinstrasse**, the old Roman north-south axis route and social pulse of the south side of the city, in its own way preserves Roman relics. The pizzerias and ice-cream parlors are in the tight grip of Italian hands. The conglomeration of people is hardly anymore lively anywhere in Cologne especially when , in front of the church, market stalls are put up. Here, exactly as on Bonner-, Alteburger-, or Merowingerstrasse, one senses the vitality of the southern part of the city: in bakeries, Italian vegetable shops; the unique environment of small booths; the kiosks where one can experience and buy almost every necessity. This can be done at any time of the day because any laws pertaining to closing times are cheerfully ignored.

In contrast, the myth of the southern part of the city is fed by other sources: in blossoms of the night and idleness; in the rituals of the pubs of the »in« groups with a higher income; or the young VW Cabriolet tourists from the surrounding villages; or the »cool cats« of the »new wave« scene with their three-day beards.

During the day, there is no trace of this. Busy life determines the course of things in this neighborhood. The neat **Balchem House** lies along the road to the Severinstor, as does the

Severinstor (Gate) at the Chlodwigplatz. Middle of the 12th century

»Invalidendom« (Invalid's »Cathedral«), a Cologne brick pub, close by the city gate. Once it was the home and inn of the Hermann distillery, an institution, which gained its nickname »Invalidendom« from the liquid mercy, which was always available here to those disappointed or mistreated in life in form of foaming Kölsch beer. The present inn »Früh em Veedel« attempts to perpetuate this nice tradition.

The **Severinstor** is one of the twelve city gates whose number is not based on traffic requirements but on symbolism. The reference »*heiliges Köln*« (holy Cologne), alludes to the city of heaven, whose golden wall described in the apocalypse had twelve gates. Although the Staufer city wall of Cologne, the largest in Europe during the Middle Ages, was not gilded nor decorated with precious stones as the city of heaven, it was so effective that the city was never conquered. However, this may not have been because of its strength but because no army was big enough to encirle the city surrounded by a wall 4.5 miles long. That the gates and the city wall fulfilled both a practical and a decorative function is evidenced by the fact that their external sides were more elaborately and painstakingly constructed than the ones facing the city.

From the Chlodwigplatz, the tour continues toward the inner city via the Ringstrasse, and soon reveals a view of the tower of the **Ulrepforte**.

The twin tower gate, early 13th century, which during the course of time has been completely changed, has an important feature – a relief picture whose original is now in the Cologne city museum. It too was restored several times and replaced by a copy. It portrays the »Battle at the Ulre Gate« in 1268, in which the archbishop made an abortive attempt to nullify the results of the community's long struggle for independence. This relief with its many figures created a century after this battle in which, according to legend, city patrons of Cologne helped to defend the city's independence, may be considered the oldest historical monument of Germany.

The extensive **Sachsenring** with its greenery is one of the best mementos of the old ring, which due to the war and reconstruction, was disfigured beyond recognition. The rooms in the remains of the city wall are tightly controlled by the *Prinzengarde* (»prince guard«). The exterior is ostentatiously neat – like a piece of the Middle Ages in a tincan. The impression variates on the basic theme of Cologne's municipal structures: forms of historic structures appear the most as fleeting flashbacks, never unified the past in quotation marks.

Diagonally across from the Finance Office, at »Am Weidenbach« is **St. Pantaleon** (Church of St. Pantaleon), another example of medieval building art, and very worth seeing.

Despite all the destruction and changes this church, dedicated to the Greek martyr Pantaleon, had to suffer, it is one of the most important structures in Cologne. The »**Westwerk**« (west side) above whose middle tower a heliograph was erected during the past century, is one of the architectural highlights of the Ottonian Archbishop Bruno, the builder, was the uncle of Emperor Otto II, whose wife, the Byzantine Princess Theophanu is buried here.

The Church of St. Pantaleon: the west façade

The Church of St. Pantaleon: pulpit, lectern, and organ in the center aisle

The west side which opens into a nave that today has again been covered with a flat roof, also lends the interior a very impressive appearance. Its square center is divided on the remaining three sides by a two-story vaulted architecture, behind which antechambers and galleries form an illuminated backdrop. The wide-spanned arches on the heavy pillars give the room an awesome tranquility; the blending of red-white colors of the pillars and arches – a classic motif of the building art of the Ottonian era creates a noble solemnity. While the lower floor of the west side also served as a baptisimal church, and for a long time, also as a parish church, the upper floor was probably primarily reserved for the imperial family. It gave the emperor a chance to participate in the service from an elevated spot. One must take into consideration that the Middle Ages saw the emperor not only as a secular power but also as a sacred power. In this respect, the »Westwerk« is to be regarded as a imperial house of God.

The view from the »Westwerk« into the nave of the church is dominated by Cologne's oldest **organ**. It is situated above the magnificent Late Gothic lectern which was created by Brabant artists at the beginning of the 16th century.

A visit to the **vault** is worthwhile because of two 12th century shrines containing religious relics. Although they cannot compete with the uniqueness of the Three Magi Shrine in the cathedral, they are excellent examples of the high level of medieval goldsmith art in the Rhine-Meuse area.

From the Ring, one drives (as quickly as possible), around the Barbarossaplatz to the Roonstrasse, which offers a fleeting but thoroughly advantageous view of the new part of Cologne. At the synagogue, the **Rathenauplatz** is one of the few spots lucky enough to have been preserved as an inner-city park as originally planned by the city architect Stübben.

Immediately after passing under the Federal Railway tracks, the Lindenstrasse leads through green meadows which open a view of the academic side of Cologne. The university stretches from the faculty for economics and sociology to the Uni-Center – study facilities for about 60,000 students.

The Kanalstrasse quickly brings one to the East-Asian Museum, at times so quickly that one must be careful not to miss the entrance to the parking area on the right side of the road.

Cologne, with its much-visited museum complex between the cathedral and the river, has probably the most extensive and newest museums in post-war Germany. However, it also has the **Museum für Ostasiatische Kunst** (Museum of East-Asian Art),

Oasis of Art and Coffee: The Museum für Ostasiatische Kunst at the Aachener Weiher (pond)

unnoticed by the broad masses. An architectural jewel, it is one of the most successful achievements of museum construction, which is more and more appreciated not only by architects and art historians. The Japanese architect Kunio Mayekawa, who studied under Le Corbusier among others, is one of the most influential representatives of modern architecture in Japan. He created a low, yet restrained structure of inter-connected laced blocks which does not interfere with the city silhouette with any unsuitable vertical accents but blends remarkably into the scenic surroundings. The gold-brown tiles, fired in Japan, clothing the building, form a harmonic contrast to the sparingly-used gray of some of the stone parts.

The water of the Aachener Weiher (pond), piped directly to the museum and above all, the Japanese garden in the inner court, create an atmosphere of the Far East. The illuminated exhibit rooms, accessible from the large foyer, seem to flow into each other. Their diverse environments are highlighted and subtly differentiated by controlled lighting, making the visual presentation of the precious inventory thoroughly effective.

To sit in the pleasant cafeteria by the water or to walk around the pond are rejuvenating interludes in the program.

The Richard-Wagner-Strasse joins the Rings again at Rudolfplatz, an area whose structures were recently slightly improved. Now that subway construction between Christophstrasse and Zülpicher Platz has been completed, the sidewalks have generally been broadened, newly landscaped, paved and flanked by bicycle paths. Above all of this, the fake historic street lanterns shine at night and remind one of the good old days.

3 Naturally only slightly. That the Rings represented at the turn of the century the stately expression of the then burgeoning industrial era, that it was a boulevard with cozy little spots, fountains, and impressive green-houses and monuments: very little can be sensed of this today. War and reconstruction have made the aesthetic quality as well as the social function of this avenue largely unrecognizable. Important public buildings from the eras of Historism and Neo Baroque, like the Hohenstaufenbad (baths) or the old opera house, disappeared from the face of the earth.

Hansa-Hochhaus (Skyscraper) 1924/25 by Jakob Koerfer

Golden Era: Hohenzollernring around 1902. Photograph

Although these old squares are still referred to as »Platz« (plaza), they are in reality intersections.

Only the reconstructed **Kaiser-Wilhelm-Ring** brings back a little of the urban flair with landscaping: a pond and fountain, narrow foot paths and a little »Bridge of Sighs«.

A few of the old villas in their new splendor, once so numerous along the Rings because it was mostly the wealthy citizens who resided here, stand in review along the Hansaring. Here and there, larger historical monuments have survived such as remains of the city wall, or the Neo Gothic Hansa Gymnasium (high school), built during the 20s, and the **Hansa-Hochhaus** (Hansa Skyscraper) once of the highest building in Europe.

Shortly before arriving at the Ebertplatz, the Lübecker Strasse branches off to the right and runs towards the Eigelsteintorburg: an urban counterpoint to the Severinstor. If one wants to go to the Ebertplatz, the counterpart to the Chlodwigplatz, one should circle around in order to finally make the turn into the Lübecker Strasse.

The changing names of this square reflect some of its most recent history. In 1923, it was called Platz der Republik, in 1933 Adolf-Hitler-Platz, in 1945 Deutscher Platz, and in 1950 **Ebertplatz**. During the expansion of the Nord-Süd-Fahrt (north-south drive), necessary to ease traffic congestion and the construction of the subway, the square, formerly so finely landscaped, was completely changed. Its pedestrian zone unfortunately lowered, was sunk more. In short, removed from the grounds.

The elegant shape of the domineering heptagonal so-called »Ringturmhaus« (Ring Tower House), called »Pencil« in slang or »Gelonida« (because of its tablet-shaped foundation) finds a counterpart in the unusual fountain by the metal sculptor Wolfgang Göddertz. Around a bundle of vertical pipes, large metal plates of various sizes are arranged in a circle at varying distances. Under high pressure the water is sprayed against them and deflected toward the middle, creating a fine fan of spray.

What the Severinstrasse is to the south of Cologne, the **Eigelstein** is to the north. Many similarities come to mind. Fans of both camps vie to make their points: flair, settings, integration of foreigners, Cologne lifestyle. Who has more to offer? Does the Roman-Italian style carry more weight, or the Turkish in Cologne's »Little Istanbul« around the Weidengasse?

At the end of Marzellenstrasse, on the left side of the street, one can see a truly dissimilar pair of buildings: the spirited façade of the Jesuit church **St. Mariä Himmelfahrt** (Church of the Assumption of the Blessed Virgin), which combines Romanesque, Gothic and Baroque forms, consciously documenting the continuity and strength of Christian tradition, and a raven black block of offices, which seems to be on an aesthetic warpath with the church.

The last day in Cologne should end outside the car on a final, short walk. The car is parked in one of the garages around the cathedral.

From the Wallrafplatz, one comes quickly to the **Museum für Angewandte Kunst** (Museum of Applied Arts). Its new home is the former Wallraf-Richartz-Museum building, a modest structure of brick built by Rudolf Schwarz in 1957. Konrad Adenauer, then mayor of Cologne, contemptuously called it a »*Mehlfabrik*« (flour factory). A secluded footpath goes around the museum, past the remains of a Roman aqueduct and a few pictoresquely placed sarcophagi, to the statue of Adolf Kolping, the socially involved churchman and »*Gesellenvater vom Rhein*« (journeyman father from the Rhine). In 1980, the pope visited also his grave in the adjacent **Minoritenkirche** (Minoriten Church). The Gothic basilica is also the burial church for Johannes Duns Scotus, theologist of the Franciscan Order.

Vis-à-vis the »*Gesellenvater*« work the journalistic mothers of the German women's movement in the editorial offices of »Emma« magazine, a leading publication for women in West Germany.

Market on the Sudermanplatz (near Ebertplatz)

Anyone who wants to go over to the opera building at the end of Kolumbastrasse must first, with much patience and baited breath, venture across the automobile »race track« known as the Nord-Süd-Fahrt (north-south drive). The thoroughfare, created during the reconstruction, cuts through the city and offers some metropolitan, but certainly not urbane perspectives. The buildings of the **WDR** (West German Broadcast) run in an east-west direction for almost one third of a mile as a dominating, although not always fortuitousley, and vexing aspect of Cologne's inner city.

The largest and by far most elegant of this building group is the so-called »Vierscheibenhaus« (Four Panel House) on the south side of the Appellhofplatz. It was erected according to plans by Helmut Hentrich: four white »panels« of different sizes alternately placed side by side, separated by dark strips. Not only the uniform windows within a well-proportioned fine screen structure but also the slight tapering toward the narrow ends, contribute to the elegance of this architecture. Above all, the fact that the light-colored body of the building does not rest on the ground, but almost seems to float on darker supports, gives this 550 feet-long building an almost happy character.

In contrast the Archivhochhaus (Archive Skyscraper), at 190 feet high the highest building of the WDR, built across the Nord-Süd-Fahrt, looks gloomy and clumsy. In view of this gigantic building group, it is difficult to imagine that, in earlier times, the WDR was lodged for more than two decades in a rather small since demolished house on the Dagobertstrasse.

Offenbachplatz, unfortunately located next to and still open to the noises of the Nord-Süd-Fahrt, offers two »musts« to Cologne tourists: the rebuilt »**Glockengasse 4711**«, and the **Opera**.

At the Rudolfplatz, on the site of the Neo Baroque opera house, destroyed during World War II, the new opera house was built according to plans by the Cologne architect Wilhelm Riphahn. He was considered the Rhineland's most important representative of the so-called »New Construction« of the 20s. Opera performances held years after the war in the auditorium of the university

Oper (Opera House, 1954–57; Architect: Wilhelm Riphahn)

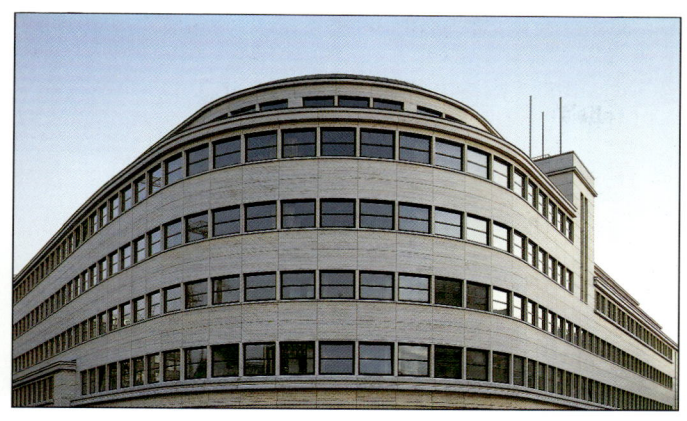

»Clear the decks!«: The Dischhaus on the Brückenstrasse

came to an end. The opera house, crowning achievement in the life of Riphahn, was opened in 1957 and was the target of both harsh criticism and high praise. »Tombstone of the Unknown Conductor« or »Pedestal for Adenauer's Statue» – by such comments and in other ways too Cologne wit took possession of the colossal new edifice.

Its distinct appearance, dictated by the functions of the individual parts of the building, is dominated by two oblique 120 feet-high towers with storage space, work shops, and offices which enclose and dominate the cubical section of the main stage. The auditorium, from the form and material clearly an autonomous building, with foyers and an auditorium divided by hanging loges, are prime example of both the reserved as well as playful elegance of architecture of the 1950s.

An older piece of Cologne architectural history is found on the way back to the church of St. Kolumba – the **Dischhaus**, a dynamic building projecting the pride of an ocean liner on its maiden voyage.

Across from it is a real gem of Cologne church art – **St. Kolumba**, a church whose original building was totally destroyed during the war and later reconstructed by Gottfried Böhm. Miraculously, a madonna was undamaged, and because of her, the new building was named »Maria in den Trümmern« (Mary in the Ruins). It houses objects worth seeing: a medieval pietà; windows by Georg Meistermann and a round window by Jan Thorn Prikker; »Antonius Praying to the Fish« by Ewald Mataré, and the tabernacle by Elisabeth Treskow.

3

Street Festival on the Roncalliplatz at the Cologne Cathedral

Directly behind the church ruins, the newly created Kolumbahof (court) runs back to the Minoritenstrasse, which joins the Hohe Strasse on the right. Shortly before the Wallrafplatz comes the **Stollwerck-Passage** with its finely kept exterior – the first of its kind in Cologne, it is an architectural overture to the once noble Hohe Strasse.

Where else but on the already familiar Roncalliplatz could the days in Cologne end? This should be done in style, i. e., in the immediate neighborhood of the central cathedral, and yet far enough away for observation. The ideal place is the terrace of the Dom-Hotel where, especially during good weather, a variety of people hustle and bustle around the cathedral where the peal of bells and the rattle of skateboards sound in unison. Heaven knows: Freakies and Fathers, the spirit of the evening and of Europe could not be any closer than here. And it is exactly that which has much to do with this ancient and modern Cologne.

VII Excursions

Altenberg Cathedral

An afternoon in Altenberg gives the visitor a chance for something like a hop- skip- and jump excursion: an unusual church, all kinds of woods for rejuvenating walks, and sumptuous waffles – with sour cherries and whipping cream – the specialty of the »Bergische Land«.

The **Altenberg Cathedral**, a Gothic Cistercian abbey of the 13th/14th century, impresses with its interior, and above all, with the largest church window in Germany and its outstanding glass painting. The church is open daily from 7 a. m. (Sat 10 a. m.) until dusk. A cathedral guide is available. For arrangements, please call 02202/78342.

In the immediate neighborhood of the cathedral is the starting point of numerous circular **hiking routes**. The pictoresque **Märchenwald** (Fairy-Tale Forest) is an enjoyment for children.

The **Gartenrestaurant Altenberger Hof** in the old Cistercian cloister opposite the church was restored in accordance with historical models. It takes care of the physical well-being of the excursionists. Daily from 6:30 a. m. to midnight.

Getting to Altenberg: Depending upon traffic, it can take a little more than three quarters of an hour by **car** from Cologne to Altenberg. From the Messe (Fair Grounds) in Deutz, take A 3 in direction of Düsseldorf to the Cologne-Mülheim exit. From there, follow the road signs toward Odenthal/Altenberg. – From the cathedral, follow the Rhine bank to the north, cross the Mülheimer bridge, Wiener Platz, Clevischer Ring, then take a half turn to the Berliner Strasse, then via Dünnwald, Schildgen and Odenthal to the cathedral. – By **streetcar/bus:** from the main train station, take streetcar line 5 toward Höhenhaus to the end of the line at Neurather Weg. From there, by bus line 434 to Altenberg. (They run every hour on Sat/Sun. The last bus back on Sat 5:45 p. m., on Sun 6 p. m.). If you wish to leave from the Neumarkt, take streetcar line 4 from there toward Schlehbusch as far as Höhenhaus (Neurather Weg), and from there, as described above.

Augustusburg and Falkenlust Castles in Brühl

An especially attractive destination near Cologne are the castles near Brühl, which one can easily visit on an afternoon excursion. **Schloss Augustusburg**, 5040 Brühl, Tel. 02232/42471, Tues–Sat 9 a.m.–noon, 1:30–4 p.m.; Closed during state receptions and in December/January.

The Baroque castle, where the elector Clemens August von Wittelsbach (1723–61) resided, was erected in 1725–68, is a former moated castle. Especially worth seeing is the **staircase** by Balthasar Neumann, the portraits of the Wittelsbach family, as well as the castle park, modeled on Versailles. Now and then, it is used for state receptions and concerts (see castle concerts, p. 122). From here it is no more than 15 minutes to **Falkenlust Castle**, the hunting lodge and refuge of electors. On the return to Augustusburg, the **castle café** offers a chance for a royal reward.

Getting to Brühl: To get there is a child's play. – By **car**: B 265, (the extension of Luxemburger Strasse) toward Zülpich to Brühl, and from there, follow the road signs to the castle. – By **streetcar/bus**: take streetcar line 18 from the cathedral/main train station toward Bonn to Brühl, and from there take bus line 706 toward Wesseling to Brühl train station. – By **train**: From the Cologne main train station to Brühl train station.

Bonn and the Rhineland

Route: Bonn – Bad Godesberg – Mehlem – Königswinter – Siebengebirge – Oberdollendorf – Schwarzrheindorf

Cologne, the dominating metropolis on the Rhine, is now and then inclined to lord it over the neighboring towns. Düsseldorf, the great rival to the north, »The Daughter of Europe« as it likes to regard itself, has the tradition of not leaving that challenge unanswered.

As far as Bonn is concerned, Cologne hardly feels anything competitive, but rather fosters the patriarchal attitude that Bonn is actually a suburb of Cologne, »small, warm, and with the shades down«. That's how the people of Cologne like to envision the appealing neighbor in the south who actually sits at the doorstep, separated by just a few Autobahn minutes.

A visitor to Cologne should use this proximity if he desires to go beyond the cathedral city for a closer look at Bonn, Bad Godesberg, and Siebengebirge, Rhine and wine. The following route presents cultural, scenic, and gastronomic delicacies for an agreeable menu of the day.

Everything points to the **Bonner Marktplatz** (Market Place) as the best place to start the day. The **Rathaus** (City Hall) with its open twin staircase and magnificent attic roof, is ornate, a spectacular Late Baroque building. It provides an effective back-drop for the vegetable and fruit market, held there during weekends. The lively and loud activities impressively demonstrate the basically southern temperament of the Rhineland.

Not far away is the **Münsterplatz** where past and present meet. It is dominated by the **Martinsmünster** (Martin Cathedral) whose predecessor allegedly dates back to Helena, mother of Emperor Constantine. Today's building, a three-aisle basilica with a transept, an elongated east choir flanked by two towers, and a mighty octagonal sqare tower, is a high point of Romanesque architecture in the Rhineland.

The façades on the square, which were recently re-designed, are cautiously trying to relate to the architecture of the cathedral, without surrendering their own individuality. The **post office**, built during the 18th century by the then deacon of the monastery,

Market Place and City Hall in Bonn

Bonn Cathedral

provides a colorful accent and a splendid background for the **Beethoven monument** erected in 1845.

In **Bad Godesberg**, a view of the architecture around the Kurpark, especially of the **Redoute**, is indeed worthwhile. The Kurhaus, a building erected during the 18th century in the style of an elector's garden castle, is today a preferred location for diplomatic and cultural events. It is the place where once the young Beethoven was introduced to Joseph Haydn and also played for him.

Via Rüngsdorf, past the American embassy, one arrives at **Mehlem** and the **Weinhäuschen** (Wine Tavern) situated directly on the Rhine vis-à-vis the Drachenfels (Dragon Rock). One can both sit comfortably on its terrace for a lunch break and also walk for hours from there south along the river to the island of Nonnenwerth.

A few hundred yards from the Mehlemer Weinhäuschen, a car ferry runs downstream on the Rhine to **Königswinter**. Above this attractive little town backed by the scenery of the Siebengebirge (Seven Hills), is the Drachenfels. Local residents ironically call it the Netherlands highest mountain because of all the visitors who come from that flat neighboring country.

However, to experience genuine Rhenish flair, one should take a sunny afternoon (if possible not on a weekend) and go to the idyllic **Oberdollendorf**. There, at the feet of the northernmost German vineyard, is the garden of the **Weingut Sülz**. One may sit and savor a bottle of the domestic »Laurentiusberg« or »Sülzenberg«.

Before returning to Cologne, there is still one more treat of a different kind to be enjoyed: the twin church in **Schwarzrheindorf**. This former castle chapel, erected in the shape of a cross, is despite its modest dimensions, a truly regal building. It belongs among the most beautiful works of Romanesque architecture. The upper part of the church was reserved for the lord of the castle during services while the lower part was for the retainers.

Gallery Bredershof and Wine Tavern in Niederdollendorf

View across the Rhine Isle Nonnenwerth to the Mountains of the Eifel

This mid-12th century building is the work of builder Arnold von Wied, cathedral provost and later archbishop of Cologne, as well as chancellor for King Konrad III. The elaborate Romanesque ceiling- and wall-frescos are based upon the visions of the prophet Ezekiel.

Information for the Day:

Route:

Cathedral-Rhine bank – traffic circle south – Autobahn Cologne-Bonn (before Bonn, get into left lane: Bonn-Zentrum) – traffic circle Bonn, from there follow the sign »Zentrum«: via the Vorgebirgsstr., Hochstadenring/Kaiser-Karl-Ring left, on Kölnstr. on the right to the parking garage »Stiftsgarage« (Park).

Continue in the same direction: Bonngasse (Beethovenhaus and Baroque façade of the Namen-Jesu-Kirche) to the **Marktplatz/Rathaus** (Market Place/City Hall), and from there to the **Münster** (Cathedral) and back.

From the parking garage to the Bertha-von-Suttner-Platz, past Oxfordstr. on the left, immediately turn right into the Belderbergstr.: through the Koblenzer Tor (gate) of the university, past the Hofgarten, ministries, Koenig Museum, Palais Schaumburg to **Godesberg**. Right after the underpass, then turn left into the Koblenzer Str., Kurpark on the right, Kurfürstenallee on the left, and park at the **Redoute**.

Continue the drive via the Kurfürstenallee, pass Friedrich-Ebert-Str. on the left, B9 (Koblenzer Str.) on the right, and soon afterwards turn left (Rüngsdorf), Kapellenweg, cross the railroad tracks, turn right on Konstantinstr., drive down the Deichmannsaue on the left, via the Austrasse into Brunhildstr./Utestr., then turn left to the Fährstr., and at the end left again (Attention: this time against traffic): sign »**Weinhäuschen**«. Park here or directly at the Rhine (following little lane by the sign).

Back to Austrasse and right to the ferry. In **Königswinter** to the Hauptstr. and left (north), through the village to

Twin Church Schwarzrheindorf

the church in **Niederdollendorf**; in front of it to the Heisterbacher Str. to **Oberdollendorf**, left on Cäsariusstr., right on Bachstr. to its end: the vineyards at **Weinhaus Gut Sülz**. (From here there is a path, about 1 1/4 miles through the vineyards).

Bachstr., Cäsariusstr. over the Grünen Weg, and after crossing the Autobahn, right to the Königswinterer Str. through **Beuel**, left on Stiftsstr. to the **Schwarzrheindorf** church.

From the parking lot of the church, follow the Autobahn sign. To return to the cathedral in Cologne, turn into Köln-Süd (Cologne south); to go to the Deutzer side, turn by the white Cologne-Bonn airport sign. (Round trip of about 60 miles; travelling time about 2½ hours).

Mehlemer Weinhäuschen (Wine Tavern)
Fährstr. 26
5300 Bonn 2 (Bad Godesberg)
Tel. 0228/342235
Except in Dec., open daily after 2 p.m.; Closed Mon
Cozy restaurant directly at the Rhine with a classic view of the Drachenfels (Dragon Rock) and the Siebengebirge (Seven Hills).

Weinhaus Gut Sülz
Bachstr. 157
Königswinter-Oberdollendorf
Tel. 02223/24178
Tues-Fri 4 p.m.–midnight; Sat, Sun and on holidays 3 p.m.–midnight; Closed Mon

Doppelkirche St. Klemens (Twin Church)
Schwarzrheindorf (near Brühl)
Tel. 0228/461609
Lower church: daily 9 a.m.–6 p.m.
Upper church/gallery, Sat 9 a.m.–6 p.m., Sun noon–6 p.m.

Weinhaus Muffendorf
Muffendorfer Hauptstr. 37
5300 Bonn 2 (Bad Godesberg)
Tel. 0228/330239
Daily noon–3 p.m. (by reservation), 6 p.m.–1. a.m.
Good place for gourmets.

VIII Service Section

Arriving in Cologne

Although the folk poet Willi Ostermann wrote a sentimental song about a Cologne native, plagued by homesickness, whose refrain is, »... *ich möch ze Foss no Kölle jonn.*« (I would like to return to Cologne on foot) – most visitors to Cologne approach the cathedral city by faster means of transportation.

Daily, the **Bundesbahn** (Federal Railroad), carries 120,000 travellers to the centrally located **main train station**. Train connections with a direct tie-in to the international train network are available around the clock. Car caravans stop in Cologne-Deutz. During trade fairs, additional connections from the main train station to Cologne-Deutz are offered.

If you go by **car**, the **Cologne Autobahnring** will get you to all parts of the town and into its center. The Autobahns come from all directions and have signs showing the respective exits.

Planes arrive at the **Köln/Bonn Airport**, 9.3 miles south-east of Cologne. Taxis and busses to the Fair Grounds and/or the inner city are available. Airport transfer service from the Cologne main train station/cathedral square to the Cologne airport: by bus (No. 170) every 20 min. Time: from 6 a.m.–10:30 p.m.; Ticket: 7,20 DM; Travel time: about 25 min.; Taxi fare, about 35 DM; Travel time: 15–20 min. A bus with the sign »Köln Messe« leaves the **Flughafen Düsseldorf** from terminal 2; charge: 16 DM.

One can also dock in Cologne. The neat, white passenger **ships** of the »Köln-Düsseldorfer« (KD), coming from Rotterdam or Basel, anchor at the Cologne docks.

Information/Important Telephone Numbers

Tourist Office
Unter Fettenhennen 19 (cathedral square/opposite the west side of the cathedral)
5000 Cologne 1
Tel. 0221/2213345
Tx 8883421 toc
Business hours: Mon–Thurs 8:30 a.m.–4 p.m., Fri 8:30 a.m.–noon

Special Services:
– Hotelroom reservations (information/booking in writing):
Tel. 2213311
– Private rooms (only during the Trade Fair seasons):
Tel. 2213335
– Tour guide: Tel. 2213332
– Special programs:
Tel. 2213388/3397

Information/Important Telephone Numbers/Shopping

Information Bureau:
(only tourist information about the city/room arrangements for the same day)
Winter: daily 8 a.m.–9 p.m., Sun and holidays 9:30 a.m.–7 p.m.
Summer: Daily 8 a.m.–10:30 p.m., Sun and holidays 9 a.m.–10:30 p.m.

Newspapers

Daily newspapers: *Kölner Stadt-Anzeiger,*
Kölnische Rundschau,
Express.
City magazines (incl. calendar of events):
Köln im..., Stadtrevue, Kölner Illustrierte, Prinz, memory

Important Telephone Numbers
(area code of Cologne is 0221)

Medical Emergency 720772
Emergency Service 11500
Taxi 2882
Federal Railroad Information (Central Travel Information) 19419
Airport Information 02203/402222
Theater and Concert Programs 11517
Movie Theater Program 11511
Exhibits, Fairs and other Events 11516
Ticket Reservation
Advance sale of theater and concert tickets: Kaufhof/Schildergasse 216692/217692
Neumarkt/subway 214232
Rudolfplatz/An d'r Hahnepooz 246945
Saturn/Hansaring 97121912
Advance ticket sales Cologneticket/Philharmonic 233854

Lost and Found Bureau 2216312
Telephone Information National 1188, International 00118

Shopping

Shopping Avenues/Centers:

Hohe Strasse/Schildergasse
Cologne's two main shopping streets run from the cathedral plateau to the Neumarkt.

Breite Strasse
Only partly car-free but a throughly quiet shopping street.

Bazaar de Cologne
Mittelstrasse
Roofed shopping center: fashions, shoes, accessories, furniture stores, restaurants, snack bars (see Route Day 2).

Ringe (Rings)
Between Zülpicher Platz and Christophstr.

Ladenstadt (Glockengasse, opposite the opera house)
Colonge's first shopping center, dating from the 60s. Parking garage.

Ehrenstrasse
Right and left, gaudy boutiques with flipped-out fashions for teenagers and early twenties. In between are »in« cafés.

St.-Apern-Strasse and Kreishausgalerie
An accumulation of art and antique stores. (Please compare with »Two Art Quarters at Your Service!«, p. 22, and Route Day 2).

Shopping

Department Stores:

Kaufhof
Bordered by the Schildergasse, Hohe Str., Cäcilienstr.
Building from 1912–14 in the classicist style, (former Tietz Department Store, then the first modern department store in Germany). Its food section enjoys the reputation of being a gourmet's paradise. However, one should not go there on Sat because of overcrowding.

Karstadt
Breite Str. 103
Recently connected to the shopping center Olivandenhof by a passage in Post-Modern style.

Special Shops:

Keramik Weber
Gürzenichstr. 16
Besides souvenirs and Rhenish stoneware, it carries ceramics from all over Europe.

Josef Feinhals Zigarren
Hohe Str. 116
Cologne's oldest specialty shop (since 1861). 1,000 different kinds of cigars.

Tonger
Am Hof 3 (Heinzelmännchenbrunnen/cathedral)
Time-honored »House of Music«. In addition to records, it carries instruments, sheet music and a rare books dept.
(See Route Day 2)

Zauberkönig
Grosse Budengasse 3
Toys, party favors.

Dieter Hohmann
art + reprogalerie
Ladenstadt
Posters, placards, art prints.

Walther König Postkarten
Breite Str. 93
Anything from the most original greeting cards to art postcards.

Cölner Teehaus
Benesisstr. 53 (near Mittelstr.)
Large selection of teas and wines.

Spielbrett
Ehrenstr. 39
Large selection of games as well as other trifles which make the heart happy.

Käsehaus Wingenfeld
Ehrenstr. 90 (corner Friesenwall)
Number one store for cheeses in Cologne with 300 different kinds.

Bäckerei Zimmermann
Ehrenstr. 75
Fragrant bread boutique. Regarded by many people of Cologne as THE baker.

Pesch
Kaiser-Wilhelm-Ring 22
Leading furniture store in the Rhineland

Saturn
Hansaring 97 (in and around the Hansa skyscraper)
Electric appliances, photo, video, Hifi, records. Low prices.

Shopping/Galleries/Art Dealers

Bookstores:

Bücherstube am Dom
Zeppelinstr. (near Neumarkt)

Buchhaus Gonski
Neumarkt 18a (passage)

Neumarkt Passage

Mayersche Buchhandlung
Neumarkt 1
(close to Schildergasse)
(See Information Day 2)

Buchhandlung Herder
Komödienstr. 11
(near the cathedral)

Köselsche Buchhandlung
Roncalliplatz 2
(cathedral plateau)
Emphasis: archeology, prehistoric history, special catalogue of literature of antiquity.

Walther König Buchhandlung
Ehrenstr. 4 (near Neumarkt)
One of the internationally leading art bookstores. Modern secondhand department.

Cologne Weekly Markets
(inner city)
Apostelnkloster (St. Aposteln)
Tues, Fri 7 a.m.–1 p.m. – a sad performance for a city of almost one million residents.

Galleries/Art Dealers

For more information about these shops see »Two Art Quarters at Your Service!«, p. 22

Galleries:

Inge Baecker
Zeughausstr. 13
Tel. 24 06 26
Tues–Fri 10 a.m.–1 p.m., 3–6 p.m., Sat 10 a.m.–1 p.m.

Daniel Buchholz
Venloer Str. 21
Tel. 52 64 12
Tues–Fri 10 a.m.–1 p.m., 3–6 p.m., Sat 10 a.m.–1 p.m.

Gmurzynska
Goethestr. 67
Tel. 23 66 21
Mon–Fri 2–6 p.m.

Karsten Greve
Wallrafplatz 3
Tel. 21 39 21
Mon–Fri 10 a.m.–1 p.m., 2:30–6:30 p.m., Sat 10 a.m.–2 p.m.

Max Hetzler
Venloer Str. 21
Tel. 52 78 53
Tues–Fri 10 a.m.–1 p.m., 3–6 p.m., Sat 10 a.m.–1 p.m.

Galleries/Art Dealers

Holtmann
Richartzstr. 10
Tel. 21 51 50
Mon–Fri 10 a.m.–1 p.m., Sat 10 a.m.–1 p.m.

Jablonka
Venloer Str. 21
Tel. 52 68 67
Mon–Fri 10 a.m.–1 p.m.,
3–6:30 p.m., Sat 10 a.m.–2 p.m.

Kicken-Pauseback
Bismarckstr. 50
Tel. 51 50 05
Tues–Fri 10 a.m.–1 p.m.,
3–6 p.m., Sat 10 a.m.–2 p.m.

Orangerie Reinz
Helenenstr. 2
Tel. 23 46 84
Tues–Fri 9 a.m.–1 p.m., 2–6.30 p.m., Sat 9 a.m.–2 p.m.

Pentagon
Bismarckstr. 50
Tel. 52 86 08
Tues–Fri 10 a.m.–1 p.m.,
Sat 10 a.m.–2 p.m.

Reckermann
Albertusstr. 16
Tel. 21 20 64
Tues–Fri 10 a.m.–6 p.m.,
Sat 10 a.m.–2 p.m.

Galerie Der Spiegel
Bonner Str. 328
Tel. 38 57 99
Mon–Fri 10 a.m.–1 p.m., 3–6 p.m.,
Sat 10 a.m.–1 p.m.

Stolz
Am Römerturm 15
Tel. 23 72 81
Tues–Fri 11 a.m.–6 p.m.,
Sat 11 a.m.–2 p.m.

Tengelmann
St.-Apern-Str. 21
Tel. 23 11 33
Tues–Fri 10 a.m.–1 p.m., 3–6 p.m.,
Sat 10 a.m.–1 p.m.

Cologne Art Market in the Deutzer Fair Halls

Galleries/Art Dealers/Money/Post Office/Climate

Wentzel
St.-Apern-Str. 26
Tel. 24 24 00
Tues-Fri 10 a.m.–1 p.m.,
Sat 10 a.m.–1 p.m.

Michael Werner
Gertrudenstr. 24–28
Tel. 21 06 61
Tues–Fri 10 a.m.–1 p.m.,
Sat 10 a.m.–2 p.m.

Zwirner
Albertusstr. 18
Tel. 23 58 37
Mon–Fri 10 a.m.–1 p.m.,
3–6:30 p.m., Sat 10 a.m.–1 p.m.

Art Dealers:

Apicella
Spichernstr. 8
Tel. 52 52 59
Tues–Fri 11 a.m.–1 p.m.,
2:30–6:30 p.m., Sat 11 a.m.–2 p.m.

Boisserée
(See Information Day 3)

Dietze
Am Römerturm 1
Tel. 21 84 02
Mon–Fri 11 a.m.–1 p.m., 3–6 p.m.,
Sat 11 a.m.–1 p.m.

Carola van Ham
Drususgasse 1–5
Tel. 23 81 37
Old, modern, and non-European art; antiques, auctions.

Lempertz
Neumarkt 3
Tel. 23 68 62
Renowned auction house: old, modern, and East-Asian art.

Rotmann
St.-Apern-Str. 9
Tel. 21 55 18
Mon–Fri 10 a.m.–1 p.m., 3–6 p.m.,
Sat 10 a.m.–2 p.m.

Sotheby's Deutschland
St.-Apern-Str./Kreishausgalerie
Tel. 23 52 84

Venator & Hanstein
Cäcilienstr. 48
Tel. 23 29 62
Second-hand, books and graphics auctions.

Weber
Gertrudenstr. 29
Tel. 21 15 42
Mon–Fri 9 a.m.–1 p.m., 3–6 p.m.,
Sat by appointment

Money/Post Office

Office Hours of Banks and Savings Banks:
Mon–Fri 8:30 a.m.–4 p.m., Thurs open till 5 p.m.

Currency Exchange Office in the Main Train Station:
Daily 7 a.m.–9 p.m.

Post Office Hours:
Mon–Fri 8 a.m.–6 p.m.,
Sat 8 a.m.–noon

Post Office at the Main Train Station:
Mon–Sat 7 a.m.–10 p.m.,
Sat 10 a.m.–10 p.m.

Climate

Due to the basin of the Cologne bay humid climate during sum-

Climate/Cologne Statistics/Museums

mer with moderate temperatures. Mild, wet winters. Despite predominant west winds, it is often misty. Coldest month: January (average temperature 2 °C); Warmest month: July (average temperature 18.7 °C).

Cologne Statistics

Age: 2,000 years
Population: 928,309 (census taken in 1987). Largest city in North Rhine-Westphalia, fourth largest city of the Federal Republic of Germany
Area: 156 square miles, (23 % recreational areas, 55 % natural and agricultural, woods, meadows, etc.)
Cars: 400,000
Bridges: 8
Newspapers: 3 daily newspapers, 5 city magazines
Media: 5 radio and TV stations (WDR, BFBS, DW, DLF, RTL plus)
Non-German population: 14.2 %
Churches: 225 (145 catholic, 80 protestant)
Kölschkneipen (Cologne pubs): 2,000
74 employees, work on the maintenance of the cathedral
Galleries: c. 130
30 museums, 1 art hall, 1 art association
6 foreign cultural institutes
30 international professional fairs
20 million tourists and visitors to the fairs annually
About 1,100 taxi cabs available around the clock
2 million »Jecken« celebrate carnival in Cologne.
100 carnival clubs and countless sport associations, private clubs, bowling organizations, and schools take part in the parades.
Consumption of Cologne beer: annually 140 liters per resident
15 kinds of Kölsch beer
2,000 seats in the Philharmonic Hall
The 600 year-old Albertus-Magnus-University has about 60,000 students.
Hotels and boarding houses: 239 with 16,800 beds
100,000 people walk down the Hohe Strasse every day.
24 million records annually (EMI Electrola) from Cologne
300 choirs

Museums

Wallraf-Richartz-Museum/ Ludwig Museum
Roman-Germanic Museum
Cologne City Museum
Museum of Applied Arts
Museum of East-Asian Art
(See Information Days 1–3)

Rautenstrauch-Joest-Museum
Ubierring 45 (between Rhine and Chlodwigplatz)
Tel. 31 1065
Tues–Sun 10 a.m.–5 p.m. The first Wed of each month 10 a.m.–8 p.m.; Closed Mon
Guided tours: Sun 3 p.m.
Anthropology, art and culture of non-European countries. One of the largest anthropological museums in Germany founded in 1906. Temporarily lodged in the Cologne Chamber Theater since 1949.

Museums/Music

Schnütgen-Museum
Cäcilienstr. 29
Tel. 221 23 10
Tues–Sun 10 a.m.–5 p.m. The first Wed of each month 10 a.m.–8 p.m.; Closed Mon
Guided tours: Sun 11 a.m., Wed 3 p.m.
Sacred art of the early Middle Ages to Baroque. Named after Alexander Schnütgen (1843–1918) who willed his collections to the city of Cologne. Attractively housed in the former St. Cecilia church (12th century), one of the twelve Romanesque churches.

Erzbischöfliches Diözesan-Museum
(Archbishopric Diocesan Museum)
Roncalliplatz 2 (cathedral plateau)
Mon–Sat 10 a.m.–5 p.m., Sun 10 a.m.–1 p.m.; Closed Thurs
Sacred art of Cologne and the lower Rhine, from early Christianity to the 20th century. Extensive collection of coins, medals, seals, pilgrim mementos, items buried in the graves of electors under the cathedral (6th century).

Domschatzkammer
(Cathedral Treasury)
Mon–Sat 9 a.m.–4:30 p.m., Sun 12:30–4:30 p.m.
Chalices, relics, monstrances.

Josef-Haubrich-Kunsthalle
Josef-Haubrich-Hof (Neumarkt)
Tel. 221 23 35
Daily 10 a.m.–5 p.m., Tues, Fri 10 a.m.–8 p.m.
Tours: Tues, Fri 6 p.m.
Alternating exhibits of new and old art and culture, organized by the Cologne museums.

Kölnischer Kunstverein
(Cologne Art Association)
Josef-Haubrich-Hof (Neumarkt)
Tel. 22137 40
Tues–Sun 10 a.m.–5 p.m.
Closed Mon
Paintings, sculptures, photographs, video from the 20s to today, supported by membership organization, founded in 1839 as »the oldest civic initiative for the arts«.

Music

Cologne's reputation as a music city – with the so-called E-music – is primarily based upon the musical reputation of two top-notch orchestras, the radio symphony orchestra of WDR, and the Gürzenich orchestra, who perform in the studio of the radio station, in the Gürzenich, in the opera house, and naturally in the philharmonic hall which was opened in 1986.

Also, part of the musical presentations includes the lively tradition of local church music which, besides being performed in the cathedral, comes impressively to the fore in the numerous Romanesque churches. Performances by the Rhenish music conservatory, the dance forums, and diverse musical organizations, like the Rhenish chamber orchestra, the Bach society, the philharmonic choir and the Brühl

Music

castle concerts, complete the city's music program.

The entertainment branch is no less melodious: jazz, folklore, pop and rock music need not hide behind the serene sounds of classical music. At present, several hundred bands play in Cologne, groups such as the Bläck Fööss or BAP, as well as lone interpreters such as the Purple Schulz, Ina Deter, Herbert Grönemeyer, Wolf Maahn who have many fans beyond the city walls.

For schedules, see the brochure »*Musikstadt Köln*« (Music City Cologne), available at the tourist office. Ticket sales: look under »Important Telephone Numbers«

Kölner Philharmonie
Bischofsgartenstr. 1
Tel. 24 02 1 00
Number 1 concert hall in Cologne, international stars and orchestras, Cologne radio symphony orchestra, Gürzenich orchestra. Since opening in 1986 has had 1,860,000 visitors (June 1990).

Grosser Sendesaal des WDR
(Large broadcasting room of WDR)
Wallrafplatz
Tel. 22 02 1 44
Concerts of the WDR, »Serenades«, »Matinée of ballad singers« (Sun mornings).

Musikhochschule Köln
(Cologne Academy of Music)
Dagobertstr. 38
Tel. 12 40 33
Concerts performed by the students of the academy of music.

Gürzenich
Martinstr. 29–37
Tel. 22 12 3 85

Oper der Stadt Köln
(Cologne City Opera)
Offenbachplatz
Tel. 22 18 4 00
Operas of all epochs, standing ensembles, guest stars, dance forum Cologne, co-production with international stages, Mozart cycle by J. P. Ponnelle.

In addition: music in Cologne churches, see »*Musikstadt Köln*« (tourist office), »*Kirche in der City*« (churches in the city). Organ concerts in the cathedral.

**Brühler Schlosskonzerte/
Schloss Augustusburg**
(Brühl castle concerts/Augustusburg castle)
May-Sept.
Organizer: Schlossstr. 2
5040 Brühl
Tel. 0 22 32/4 31 83, 4 39 02

Jazz live:

Stadtgarten-Restaurant

Stadtgarten
Venloer Str. 40
Tel. 51 60 39
Innovative jazz, European and American musicians' scene. About 15 performances per

Music/Night Life

month. Admission free on the first Sat and third Fri of the month.

Subway
Aachener Str. 82–84
Tel. 51 79 69
Classics of jazz music. Performances at the beginning of the week, Wed–Sat disco.

Em Streckstrump
Buttermarkt 37
Tel. 21 79 50
Daily live jazz with different bands from Germany and foreign countries, Dixieland.

Rock:

Luxor
Luxemburger Str. 40
Tel. 21 95 06
20 performances a month by international rock/pop music groups.

U-Musik:

Tanzbrunnen in the Rhine park
Programs and tickets at the Cologne tourist office/ticket office at Tanzbrunnen. Performances from April to Sept.
Tel. 22 13 3 68
Folklore, jazz, rock, pop, entertainment.

Night Life

Night life in Cologne? A little art, disco hubbub, transvestite shows, live music, smoke-filled pubs and profound discussions over wine, in short, not exactly provincial, but a city of the world? Well...?

The following selection of night life is limited to a few recommendations. Not mentioned, for example, are the many places in the old part of the city where one can have a good old time, nor the bars and lounges of many large hotels where one can enjoy a good drink without any bustle.

Meeting Places on the Scene:

Alcazar
Bismarckstr. 39a
(near Friesenplatz)
Tel. 51 57 33
Noon–1 a.m., Wed, Fri, Sat open till 3 a.m.
Menu of the day and snacks.
(See »Two Art Quarters at Your Service!«, p. 22)

Alter Wartesaal
(at the main train station)
Tel. 13 30 61
4 p.m.–2 a.m. Food served from 6 p.m.–1 a.m.
A good place for a cultivated happy hour. Bar and restaurant in the waiting room, which was uniquely restored at the turn of the century.

Blue Shell
Luxemburger Str. 32
(near Barbarossaplatz)
Tel. 23 12 48
5 p.m.–1 a.m.
Young scene.

Broadway Café
Ehrenstr. 11
(near Neumarkt/Rudolfplatz)
Tel. 24 47 69
11 a.m.–1 a.m.
(See »Two Art Quarters at Your Service!«, p. 22)

Night Life

Hang-out »Blue Shell«, Luxemburger Strasse

Café Central
Jülicher Str. 1
(near Rudolfplatz)
Tel. 23 99 89
7–1 a.m. (also a restaurant)
(See »Two Art Quarters at Your Service!«, p. 22)

Chin's
Im Ferkulum 18
(south side)
Tel. 32 81 96
Noon–1 a.m., Sun 6 p.m.–1 a.m.;
Kitchen 6 p.m.–midnight
Popular meeting place on the south side of the city. Light cuisine. Reservations recommended.
(See »Two Art Quarters at Your Service!«, p. 22)

Filmdose
Zülpicher Str. 39
(near Zülpicher Platz)
Tel. 23 96 43
7 p.m.–1 a.m., Sat till 3 a.m.
Pub, cinema, little theater stage all in one. Ticket sales after 7 p.m.

Hammerstein's
Antwerpener Str. 34
(near Friesenplatz)
Tel. 51 95 96
7 p.m.–1 a.m., except Mon
Kitchen open till 12:45 a.m.
American bar, restaurant.

Hotel Timp
Neumarkt 25 (old town)
Tel. 21 22 01
11 p.m.–4 a.m.
Burlesque show after 1 a.m.

Linus
Ubierring 22 (south side)
Tel. 32 87 20
8 p.m.–1 a.m., Wed–Sat till 3 a.m.

Moderne Zeiten
Auf dem Berlich/Breite Str. 100
(near Neumarkt)
Tel. 21 15 77
8:30–1 a.m.; Kitchen till midnight
American bar, bistro, Post-Modern elegance and beautiful people.

Night Life

Opera
Alteburger Str. 1 (south side)
Tel. 32 91 87
5 p.m.–1 a.m., Fri–Sun till 3 a.m.;
Kitchen 6 p.m.–midnight
A meeting place of long standing in the city's south.

Roxy
Aachener Str. 2
(near Rudolfplatz)
Tel. 25 19 69
10 p.m.–3 a.m., Fri, Sat till 4:30 a.m., Wed–Gay Night

Schroeder's
Alteburger Str. 11 (south side)
Tel. 32 68 38
11–1 a.m.; Kitchen open 12–3 p.m., 6–11 p.m.
The »in« spot for south side of town tourists. Ice-cream parlor, tavern and restaurant, all under one roof.

Spitz
Ehrenstr. 43 (near Neumarkt)
Tel. 24 61 63
9–1 a.m., Sun 11–1 a.m.
(See »Two Art Quarters at Your Service!«, p. 22)

Bars:

Hotel Inter-Continental
Helenenstr. 14
(near St.-Apern-Str./Neumarkt)
Tel. 2 28-0
9 p.m.–3 a.m.; Closed Mon, Sun
Bar on the top floor – amazing view of the city at night.

Discos:

Alter Wartesaal
At Main Train station
Tel. 13 30 61
Mon, Fri, Sat 10 p.m.–5 a.m.
On weekends a crowded disco in the old waiting room, »Blue Monday«: something special for all who did not dance enough during the weekend.

Disco in the »Alte Wartesaal« of the Main Train Station

Night Life/Restaurants

Camayenne
Richard-Wagner-Str./Händelstr.
(near Rudolfplatz)
Daily from 9 p.m.–1 a.m.
Disco strongly frequented by
black people.

tito's
Hohenzollernring 16
(near Rudolfplatz)
Tel. 21 89 78
Fri, Sat 10 p.m.–4:30 a.m.

Zorba the Buddha
Hohenzollernring 40
(near Friesenplatz)
Tel. 12 22 09
9 p.m.–3 a.m.; Closed Mon
Bhagwan-disco all in white,
primarily a young crowd.

Cafés/Wine Taverns:
(See also Information Days 1–3)

Beiss'l
Otto-Fischer-Str. 1
(near Luxemburger Str./Barbarossaplatz/Südbahnhof
Tel. 41 25 79
Gaily decorated wine tavern.

Zur Alten Wettannahme
Alteburger Str. 16 (south side)
Tel. 31 89 30
Closed Sun
Casually elite, mostly for the fine
minded.

Settebello
Alteburger Str. 5 (south side)
Tel. 32 91 94
Ice-cream specialties, Tiramisu,
Zabaglione.

Restaurants

Reservations are recommended
for all restaurants.
The three categories refer only to
average prices for appetizers
and main course or daily menues:
Low price category: to 30 DM
Middle price category: to 45 DM
High price category: to 80 DM

Disco »Zorba the Buddha«, Hohenzollernring

Restaurants

Very high price category/Luxury restaurants: over 100 DM

Lower Price Category:

Carpaccio
Lindenstr. 5 (near Rudolfplatz)
Tel. 23 64 87
Closed Tues
Four brothers who make good Italian food and quick service. Mon, Thurs, and Fri fish plates.

Ezio
Apostelnstr. 50–52
(near Neumarkt)
Tel. 23 26 60
Closed Sun, Mon–Fri 9 a.m.–9 p.m., Sat till 5 p.m.
Exclusive snack bar.
(See »Two Art Quarters at Your Service!«, p. 22)

Mexican Manhattan
Im Ferkulum 32 (south side)
Tel. 32 86 33
Texan-Mexican food, bar with (usually) good Margaritas.

Oasis
Kennedy Ufer 1
(in the Lufthansa building)
Tel. 81 44 41
Greek restaurant at the Deutzer bank with a beautiful view of the illuminated Cologne Rhine bank in the evening.

Olé
Pfälzer Str. 1
(near Friesenplatz)
Tel. 24 43 58
Known for Spanish specialties, Paella, fish dinners.

Tchang
Grosse Sandkaul 19
(near Gürzenich/Hohe Str.)
Tel. 21 76 51
Cologne's oldest Chinese restaurant (1954). Especially recommended: roast duck with bean sprouts.

Middle Price Category:

Bistro B
Komödienstr. 52
(near Römerbrunnen)
Tel. 13 47 07
Sun, holidays, closed
Parisian bistro, little offshoot of Poele d'or. Specialty: candied poultry legs.

Bizim
Weidengasse 47
(near Eigelstein)
Tel. 13 15 81
Sun, Mon noon closed
Turkish creative kitchen, appetizer buffet, lamb specialties.

Da Tullio
Bonner Str. 328 (near Bayenthalgürtel/Marienburg)
Tel. 38 70 68
Closed Tues
(See »Two Art Quarters at Your Service!«, p. 22)

Kyo
Roonstr. 8
(near Barbarossaplatz)
Tel. 24 62 39
Japanese restaurant, Sushi

Le Moissonier
Krefelder Str. 25
(near Hansaring)

Restaurants

Tel. 72 94 79
Mon, Sun noon closed
A former winery, now a restaurant with regional French cooking, and over 45 kinds of wine, which can also be ordered by the glass.

Maharani
Hohenzollernring 53
(between Rudolf-/Friesenplatz)
Tel. 25 24 17
Indian specialty restaurant, hidden in nice backyard.

Haus Marienbild
Aachener Str. 561 (Braunsfeld)
Tel. 49 31 66
A pleasant, elegant ambience, where one can savor everything from plain cooking to lobster.

Musette
Rathenauplatz 7 (near Rudolfplatz/Hohenstaufenring)
Tel. 24 73 69
Closed Mon
Small, comfortable art-déco restaurant with slightly French cooking.

Nana's
Pfeilstr. 15 (near Rudolfplatz)
Tel. 21 14 20
Smart city restaurant with a bar next to exclusive fashion boutiques. Meals from pea soup to caviar.

Pierre
Lütticher Str. 12 (near Rudolfplatz/Hohenzollernring)
Tel. 52 54 53
Small French restaurant with a frequently changing menu.

Order from the cook! Homemade pastry and tureens.

Schnittert's
Friesenwall 29 (near Ehrenstr.)
Tel. 25 44 11
Sun and holidays closed
Nouvelle cuisine in a comfortable backyard.

Solferino
Marienburger Str. 2
(Marienburg/near Rhine bank)
Tel. 34 13 98
Closed Wed
(See »Two Art Quarters at Your Service!«, p. 22)

High Price Category:

Gasthaus Adler
Friesenwall 74 (near Ehrenstr.)
Tel. 21 71 93
Closed Mon
In a historic house, old and new are combined: German cuisine and country food with high-tech, Baden specialties like Swabian »*Maultaschen*«.

Alfredo
Tunisstr. 3 (near Opernplatz)
Tel. 23 43 01
Sat evening and Sun closed
Elegant top-notch restaurant with Italien specialties.

Amabile
Görresstr. 2 (near Rathausplatz)
Tel. 24 60 17
Reservations after 5 p.m.
French gourmet restaurant. Specialty: »lobster tail à la Cinderella«.

Restaurants

Ballarin
Ubierring 35 (between Chlod-wigplatz and Rhine)
Tel. 32 61 33
Closed Sat afternoon and Sun
Classic French cuisine in a cheerful elegant ambience without the customary frills. Specialties: Duck liver tureen, bresse pigeon au jus.

Rino Casati
Ebertplatz 3 (near Hansaring/Theodor-Heuss-Ring)
Tel. 72 11 08, 72 74 98
Closed Sun
Elegant Italien restaurant with a modern, creative kitchen. Choice fish specialties.

Daitokai
Kattenbug 2
(near city museum)
Tel. 12 00 48
Closed Sun
Excellent Japanese restaurant, Sushi.

La Baurie
Vorgebirgstr. 35
(near Sachsenring/south side)
Tel. 38 61 49
Closed Sat afternoon and Mon
Pleasant French restaurant with classical fine food, pancakes and lox.

Lini
Sachsenring 3 (south side)
Tel. 32 16 73
Closed Sat afternoon, Sun and holidays
Small restaurant with a Post-Modern atmosphere, good Italian food.

Pan e Vin
Heumarkt 75 (old town)
Tel. 24 84 10, 23 82 77
Closed Mon
Exclusive Italian bistro. Choice fish specialties.

Tomate
Aachener Str. 11
(near Rudolfplatz)
Tel. 25 29 62
Closed Sun afternoon
The red neon tomato can be seen from afar. An easy-going, comfortable little restaurant, menus change daily, new European cuisine.

Tomatissimo
Aachener Str. 21
(near Rudolfplatz)
Tel. 25 10 22
Closed Sun afternoon
Successor to Franz Keller's restaurant; bar, bistro, restaurant with semi-French cuisine. A little more expensive than the »Tomate« next door.

Trattoria Toscana
Friesenwall 44 (near Neumarkt)
Tel. 31 58 47
Closed Mon
(See »Two Art Quarters at Your Service!«, p. 22)

Very High Price Category/Luxury Restaurants:

Goldener Pflug
Olpener Str. 241 (Merheim)
Tel. 89 55 09, 89 61 24
Closed Sat afternoon, Sun and holidays

Restaurants

Not three, but just two Michelin stars crown the kitchen of the well-known restaurant.

Chez Alex
Mühlengasse 1
(near Gross St. Martin)
Tel. 230560
Closed Sat afternoon, Sun and holidays
Top-notch gourmet restaurant.

La Poele d'or
Komödienstr. 50–52
(near Römerbrunnen)
Tel. 134100
Closed Sun, Mon afternoon and holidays
French cuisine à la Bado, fine choice fish specialties, considered classical for Cologne.

Remise
Wendelinstr. 48 (Müngersdorf)
Tel. 491881
Gourmet temple; very traditional atmosphere.

Weinhaus »Im Walfisch«
Salzgasse 13 (old town)
Tel. 219575
Closed Sun and holidays
Light cuisine, choice fish specialties and shellfish elaborate wine list, historic house in the narrow alleys of the old town.

Breweries and Pubs:

Früh
Am Hof (near cathedral)
(See Information Day 1)

Früh em Veedel
Chlodwigplatz 48
(near south side)
(See Information Day 3)

Klein Köln
Friesenstr. 53
(near Friesenplatz)
Tel. 238876
(See »Two Art Quarters at Your Service!«, p. 22)

Lommerzheim
Siegesstr. 18
(near Deutzer train station)
Tel. 814392
Closed Tues
Tremendous, and with many local characters.

Malzmühle
Heumarkt (near old town)
Tel. 210117
One of the traditional Cologne breweries.

Brauhaus Päffgen
Friesenstr. 64
(See Information Day 2)

Päffgen
Heumarkt 62 (old town)
Tel. 219720
Closed Mon
Old town Cologne pub in a historic house.

Brauhaus Sion
Unter Taschenmacher 5–7
(old town)
Tel. 214203
Another traditional brewery.

Hans Töller
Weyerstr. 96
(near Barbarossaplatz)
Tel. 214086
Closed on holidays and Sun

Restaurants/Cologne Specials

An Institution in Deutz: »Lommerzheim« Inn

Historical Cologne tavern, quieter atmosphere than in the larger breweries. Tasty Rhenish home-cooking.

Beer Gardens:

Depending on the Cologne climate, they are normally open from April to September.

Stadtgarten

Venloer Str. 40
Daily 5 p.m.–midnight
(See »Two Art Quarters at Your Service!«, p. 22, and »Music«, p. 122)

Zum Treppchen

Kirchstr. 15
(Rodenkirchen/Rhine bank)
Tel. 39 21 79
Daily 10 a.m.-midnight
Known all over town, and in idyllic surroundings.

Biergarten im Volksgarten

Volksgartenstr. 27 (near Sachsenring/south side)
Tel. 38 26 26
Situated in a park by the same name, with a beautiful view of the lake. Primarily young people.

Wolkenburg

Mauritiussteinweg 59
(near Neumarkt)
Tel. 23 64 42
In summer, Mon–Sat after 5 p.m., Sun after 12 p.m.
Little beer garden in the beautiful Baroque court of a former cloister. Also the seat of the Cologne men's glee club, which is rich in tradition and known for its annual performances in the Cologne opera house during the carnival season. Trademark: Men in female roles!

Cologne Specials

The biggest specialties in Cologne – art and churches – practically leap to the eye. By contrast the smallest ones leap to the mouth.

Cologne Specials

To get a realistic taste of Cologne, one must resort to the city's eating and drinking establishments. Gourmets are warned in advance – the cuisine of the Rhineland and of Cologne does not exactly place culinary flights of fancy on the table. Its strength lies more in its solidity. For instance, the typical sandwich of Cologne, the so-called »halve Hahn« (literally half a chicken), is a roll with Dutch cheese on it.

Another local favorite is also a model of modest proportions: »Himmel un Äd« (Heaven and Earth) which consists of mashed potatoes, applesauce and a proper blood sausage. Just as hearty is the crispy »Rievkoche«, a cross between a potato pancake and hash browns. The smell of this Cologne specialty engulfs visitors coming from the main train station and casting their first sight of the Cologne Cathedral.

But modest as it may be, Cologne has made one very important contribution to the cuisine of the world – the famous *Sauerbraten*. A delicacy of international fame, *Sauerbraten* is a true emissary of Rhineland cooking at its tastiest. Here's a genuine recipe from a Cologne kitchen (see at the bottom of the page):

But what use are all the tasty local meals without the proper »juice« to hold Cologne's body and soul together, and to loosen its tongue – the *Kölsch*. Very light in alcohol, tart, and served straight from the tap, it is the »national« drink of the people of Cologne, best enjoyed from the typical slender glasses in the traditional brewery taverns (see »Breweries and Pubs«, p. 130/131) where blue-aproned waiters serve freshly tapped glassfuls.

When the offices close and the happy hour is at hand, pubs in the city begin to fill and the local heroes take their places at the bars. Naturally, this is also the best time for guests and visitors to become acquainted with the

Ingredients:	1 pound beef marinated in ¼ liter (1 cup) red wine vinegar, ¼ liter water, ¼ cup raisins, 4 peppercorns, 1–2 bay leaves for 3 days (turn occasionally)
Cooking:	Remove meat from marinade (save for later), rinse and spread it with mustard. Fry in hot fat, salting lightly. Add one sliced onion, peeled tomatoes, and one celery stalk cut in pieces. Cook slowly on low flame 30 minutes, then add one cup of crumbled rye bread crusts (or pumpernickel crumbs). Finally add ½ cup hot beef broth and reduce by simmering to half. Stir in marinade and cook another 15 minutes. If desired, thicken sauce with cornstarch or sour cream. Total cooking time: 2 hours. Serves two.

lifestyle of Cologne. Reserved more for the coffee and cake fans are the daylight hours when the sweet and tempting treasure chest of numerours cafés and bakeries can be opened. (See Information Days 1–3). Like all the »tribes« of the Rhineland, the population of Cologne has a distinct sweet tooth, cherishing its moments over a hot cup of coffee with an ardent passion.

The eats and drinks of Cologne are intended for immediate enjoyment. They're poor candidates for worldwide export to former tourists. But a touch of Cologne exists to send, to take home and to give. The »Cologne water« otherwise known all over the world under the brand name of »4711« makes for a welcome souvenir. That's 3 × Cologne – for the eye, the mouth and the nose!

Theater

Schauspielhaus
Offenbachplatz
Tel. 2218400/evening ticket office: 2218252
Closed until 1990 due for restorations. Performances in the »Theater in der Kuppel« on the Offenbachplatz in front of the playhouse.

Kammerspiele
Ubierring 45 (in the Rautenstrauch-Joest-Museum)
Tel. 2218400/evening ticket office: 327990
Repertoire from old stand-bys to modern classics.

Schlosserei im Schauspielhaus
Entrace Krebsgasse
Tel. 2218400/evening ticket office: 2218321
Theater workshop.

Theater am Dom
Glockengasse 11
(Kölner Ladenstadt)
Tel. 219921
Boulevard theater.

Theater Der Keller
Kleingedankstr. 6
(near Sachsenring/Ulrepforte)
Tel. 318059
20th century dramatists.

Volkstheater Millowitsch
Aachener Str. 5
(near Rudolfplatz)
Tel. 251747
»*Kölsche*« farces with the public's darling and honorary citizen Willi Millowitsch.

Hänneschen
Puppet Theater of Cologne
Eisenmarkt 2 (at Heumarkt)
Tel. 212095
Puppet theater for children, Wed–Sun 2:30–5p.m. and adults in a dialect that can be understood by non-Cologners.

Senftöpfchen
Grosse Neugasse 2–4
(Brügelmannhaus in the old town)
Tel. 237980
Renowned cabaret stage with a variety of programs: revue, cabaret, political satire, singers.

Die Machtwächter
Gertrudenstr. 24 (near Neumarkt)
Tel. 242101
Political cabaret since 1966.

Events

Events

Fairs:

Cologne is the show place of 30 international fairs. The most important ones are:

Internationale Möbelmesse. New Products from the international furniture industry, January

Herren-Mode-Woche. International men's fashion fair, February and August

Westdeutsche Kunstmesse (West German art fair). Art and antiques. In all even-numbered years February, alternating with Düsseldorf

DOMOTECHNIA (Domestic mechanical appliances). International fair of small and large electric household appliances, house technology and kitchens. February

Internationale Eisenwarenmesse (International iron ware fair), March

IFMA. International bicycle and motorcycle exhibit, in September during all even-numbered years

SPOGA. International fair of sporting goods, camping equipment and garden furniture, September

ANUGA. World market of nutrition. September/October during all odd-numbered years

photokina. New Products from the photo, -film-, and video branch. In October during all even-numbered years

Art Cologne. International art market, November

Other Important Local Events:

December/January
Six-Day Race in the Cologne sports arena (Fair Grounds)

February
Cologne Carnival
(Week before Ash Wednesday) Thurs: Women's carnival, opening of the street carnival on the Alter Markt (Old Market); Sun: Cologne schools and private groups parade through Cologne's inner city; Mon: Rosenmontag, last Monday before Lent, big carnival parade with the »triumphirate« – prince, farmer and virgin – through the inner city; Tues: parades through various parts of the city; Ash Wed: traditional fish dinner, beginning of Lent.

May
Mühlenheimer Gottestracht
Boat procession on Corpus Christi Day with countless boats on the Rhine. Between 11 a.m.–1 p.m.

July
International Summer Academy of Dance

August
Internationales Leichtathletik Sportfest (International track and field athletics) at Müngersdorfer stadium

September
Internationales Pantomimenfest (International Pantomime Festival), »Jugglers«

November
Cologne Jazz House Festival (Stadtgarten-City Garden)

Events/Transportation

And naturally, every other Saturday afternoon: the Müngersdorfer stadium, when the »FC«, the **1. FC Cologne** soccer team plays. Visitors to Cologne who are not 100% fans of the »*Geissbockklub*« (billy-goat club the 1. FC Cologne) should avoid the south curve in the stadium when getting admission tickets.

Churches and Art

Information about church services, speeches, tours and musical performances can be found in the brochure »*Kirche in der City*« (churches in the city), which is available in most churches, or at the Catholic city deaconry. Tel. 579090

Transportation

Cologne's **main thoroughfares** are ring or star streets. The city is encircled by semi-circles of the Autobahnring, Militärring, Gürtel, outer and inner Kanalstrasse, and the so-called Ringe, which run along the same direction as the old city wall.

The names of the star streets refer to the four directions of the compass: Aachener Strasse (west), Bonner Strasse (south) Neusser Strasse (north), etc.

Now, a computerized **parking guidance** system makes the search for parking places easier. Any parking space that is available within the three main areas: Cathedral/main train station, Neumarkt and the Rings is color marked.

Public municipal transportation is by busses and lines of the **Kölner Verkehrsbetriebe (KVB)** (Cologne transportation operation): 47 lines are available. The rates for one-way fares are scaled according to distances: a commuter ticket, valid for 24 hours: 7 DM. A commuter **ticket for 3 days** in Cologne: 13 DM. A ticket for the Cologne fair (4 trips cathedral/Cologne fair) 5.60 DM.

1,100 **taxi cabs** are available around the clock. Their stands are on all larger intersections and traffic junctions. In the inner city for example, they are at Neumarkt, Alter Markt, Waidmarkt, Philharmonie, Oper/Theater (Offenbachplatz), tourist office, cathedral (three stands), Ebertplatz, Friesenplatz, Rudolfplatz, Barbarossaplatz, Chlodwigplatz. There are also taxi stands in front of all large hotels. During the fair season, they also stop at smaller hotels. Many taxi stands in the suburbs have telephones for calling taxis.

The »*Rettungsring*« (life preserver), is a special taxi service. Anyone who is intoxicated in the evening and neither wants to sit behind the steering wheel nor leave his car behind, can call for a taxi driver who will drive his car back. Since the driver has to be brought back to his taxi by another driver, the service costs three times as much as the normal fare.

Porter service: the cab driver picks up the traveler and his luggage directly at the train platform and brings everything to wherever the traveler is staying.

Public Transportation in the Cologne Region

Solingen
Opladen
Langenfeld
Leverkusen
Schlebusch
Odenthaler Str.
Leuchterstr.
Am Emberg
Fixheider Weg
Neurather Weg
Rixdorfer Str.
Von-Sparr-Str.
Keupstr.
Montanusstr.
K-Holweide
K-Dellbrück
Duckterath
Bergisch Gladbach
S 11
Mülheimer Ring
Herler Ring
Vischeringstr.
Maria-Himmelfahrt-Str.
Neufelder Str.
Dellbrück Mauspfad
Dellbrück Hauptstr.
Thielenbruch
Wiener Platz
Wichheimer Str.
K-Mülheim
Herler Str.
Buchheim
Grünstr.
K-Buchforst
Waldecker Str.
Stegerwaldsiedlung
Messe/Sporthalle
K-Deutz
Deutz/Messe
Deutz-Kalker Bad
Kalk, Post
Kalk, Kapelle
Fuldaer Str.
Frankfurter Str.
Kalker Friedhof
Merheim
Fiehbachstr.
Brück Mauspfad
Lustheide
Refrath
Kippekausen
Frankenforst
Neuenweg
Kölner Str.
Bensberg
Deutz-Kalker Str.
Vingst
Ostheim
Suevenstr.
K-Kalk
Autobahn
Rath-Heumar
Röttgensweg
Königsforst
Steinweg
Porzer Str.
Severinsbrücke
Drehbrücke
Poller Kirchweg
Südbrücke
Krückelstr.
Poll, Salmstr.
Poll, Autobahn
Westhoven, Kölner Str.
Westhoven, Berliner Str.
Ensen, Gilgaustr.
Ensen Kloster
Porz, Steinstr.
Porz Markt
Porz Glaswerke
Tulpenweg
Zündorf
Overath
Gummersbach
Porz-Heumar
Porz-Gremberghoven
Porz (Rhein)
Porz-Wahn
Troisdorf
Siegburg
Rhein
Marienburg
Rodenkirchen
Siegstr.
Michaelshoven
Sürth
Godorf
Wesseling Nord
Wesseling
Hersel
Bonn
Commuter Train
Service starts on May 27, 1990
Streetcar
German Federal Railway Train
Airport Shuttle Bus
Park and Ride Service
Status as of Sept. 16, 1989

About the Authors:

Horst Schmidt-Brümmer, Ph.D., born 1940 in Cologne. Studied German and English philology and philosophy in Munich and Cologne. In 1970, he went to the University of California in Los Angeles as lecturer for German literature. Since 1977, he is a publisher and author in Cologne. Numerous publications about the American lifestyle as well as American travel subjects are his specialty.

Paul von Naredi-Rainer, Ph.D., born in Knittelfeld/Austria in 1950. Studied art history, music science, archaeology, and philosophy. Until 1988, director of the Rhenish picture archives in Cologne; 1982, habilitation in general art history; since 1988, professor of art history at the University of Innsbruck.

★

J. M. R. Arthur is free-lance translator in Carson City, Nevada.

Kathleen Schaefer is an American who has lived in Germany since 1969, mostly in Frankfurt and Munich. She is a free-lance translator, writer and publisher of Life in Germany Newsletter.

Gerhard Knauf, Senior Master, born 1938 in Berlin. Studied German philology and geography in Cologne. Teaches at a high school.

Christiane Vielhaber, Ph.D., born 1948 in Celle. Studied dramatics, art history, and German philology in Cologne. Works as a free-lance journalist and art critic for radio and press.

Gerta Wolff. Born 1935. After an education as a teacher and a few years in service she became a free-lancer in adult education. Publications: Das Römisch-Germanische Köln, Führer zu Museum und Stadt, Köln; St. Severin, in: Stadtspuren, Köln: Die Romanischen Kirchen, 1984.

Index

Academy of Art and Design 90
Alt St. Heribert 30, 49
Altenberg 106
Alter Markt 31, 52
An Farina 58
An Gross St. Martin 31, 51 f.
Antoniterkirche (Church) 59, 71

Bazaar de Cologne 76
Belgisches Viertel (Belgian Quarter) 22
Bismarckstrasse 24
Bottmühle 90
Brühl 107
   Augustusburg/Falkenlust Castles 107

Cathedral 9, 11, 12, 14, 15, 29, 33 ff.
   Altar of the City Patrons 12, 38
   Domplatte (Cathedral Ledge) 29
   Gero Crucifix 38
   High Choir 37
   Petersportal (Portal of Peter) 35
   Sepulchers 38
   Shrine of the Three Magi 37
Chlodwigplatz 85

Deutzer Brücke (Bridge) 30, 49 f.
Dischhaus 88, 103
Dreikönigengymnasium (Three-Magi High School) 12

Ebertplatz 86 f., 99
Ehrenstrasse 77
Eigelstein 100
Eigelsteintorburg 87, 99
Eisenmarkt 51
Erzbischöfliches Diözesan-Museum (Archbishopric Diocesan Museum) 16

Fastnachtsbrunnen (Carnival Fountain) 58, 64 f.
Fischmarkt 54
Friesenstrasse/-wall 77 f.

Glockengasse 4711 88, 102
Gross St. Martin (Church of St. Martin) 9, 11, 32, 52 ff.
Gülichplatz 58
Gürzenich 58, 65 f.
   Flight of Stairs 66

Hafenstrasse 55
Hansa-Gymnasium (High School) 86, 99
Hansa-Hochhaus (Skyscraper) 86, 99
Hauptbahnhof (Main Train Station) 20, 38
Haus Balchem 85, 92
Heinrich-Böll-Platz 39, 44
Heinzelmännchenbrunnen (Fountain of Elves) 32, 56
Heumarkt 31, 50 f.
Hohe Strasse 71, 88
Hohenzollernbrücke (Bridge) 29, 44
Hotel Maritim 30 f., 50
Hyatt Regency Hotel 30, 49

Jan-van-Werth-Brunnen (Fountain) 31, 52

Käthe Kollwitz Museum 59, 75
Köln Messe (Cologne Fair) 15, 30, 48
   Messeturm (Fair Tower) 48
Kölnisches Stadtmuseum (Cologne City Museum) 60, 80 f.

Lufthansa-Hochhaus (Skyscraper) 30, 49

Mariensäule (Mary's Pillar) 59, 79
MediaPark 16, 18
Mikwe 58, 64
Minoritenkirche (Church) 87, 100
Mittelstrasse 77
Museum für Angewandte Kunst (Museum of Applied Arts) 16, 87, 100
Museum für Ostasiatische Kunst

(Museum of East-Asian Art)　86, 96 f.
Museum Ludwig　16, 22, 29, 39 f., 44

Neumarkt　74
Neumarkt Passage　74 f.

Olivandenhof　71 f.
Oper (Opera)　87 f., 102 f.
Ostermannbrunnen (Fountain)　31, 51

Pfeilstrasse　77
Philharmonie (Philharmonic Hall)　16
Praetorium　8, 12, 58, 63

Rathaus (City Hall)　13, 58, 63 f.
　City Hall Tower　63
　Hansasaal (Hall)　64
　Löwenhof (Lion Courtyard)　64
　Ratskapelle (Chapel of the City Councillors)　12
　Renaissance Arcade　64
Rathenauplatz　96
Rautenstrauch-Joest-Museum (Ethnology Museum)　16
Rheingarten-Skulptur (Rhine Garden Sculpture)　44
Rheinland (Rhineland)　107 ff.
　Bad Godesberg　109
　Bonn　107 ff.
　Königswinter　110
　Oberdollendorf　110
　Schwarzrheindorf　110 f.
Rheinpark (Rhine Park)　30
Richmodishaus　73
Ringe (Rings)　86, 98 f.
　Sachsenring　94
　Kaiser-Wilhelm-Ring　99
Roman City Wall　60, 80 ff.
Römerbrunnen (Roman Fountain)　60, 82
Römerturm (Roman Tower)　23, 60, 79 f.
Römisch-Germanisches Museum (Roman-Germanic Museum)　15, 58, 61 ff.
　Dionysian Mosaic　15, 61
　Glass Collection　63
　Jewelry Collection　63
Roncalliplatz　104 f.
Rudolfplatz　86, 97

Schildergasse　8, 71
Severinstorburg　85, 93 f.
Severinstrasse　92
St. Alban (Church of St. Alban)　66
St. Andreas (Church of St. Andrew)　10, 60, 82 f.
St. Aposteln (Church of the Apostles)　10, 59, 75 f.
St. Cäcilien (Church of St. Cecilia)　11
St. Georg (Church of St. George)　10
St. Gereon　9, 10, 59, 78 f.
　Decagon　78
St. Kolumba (Church of St. Kolumba)　88, 103
St. Kunibert (Church of St. Kunibert)　10
St. Mariä Himmelfahrt (Church of the Assumption of the Blessed Virgin)　13, 87, 100
St. Maria im Kapitol (Church of St. Mary in the Capitol)　11, 58 f., 66 ff., 75
　Dreikönigspförtchen (Three-Magi Gate)　59, 66
　Lichhof　59, 66
　Three-Conch Choir　70
St. Maria Lyskirchen (Church of St. Mary Lyskirchen)　11
St. Pantaleon (Church of St. Pantaleon)　9, 11, 85 f., 94 ff.
St. Severin (Church of St. Severin)　10, 85, 91 f.
St. Ursula (Church of St. Ursula)　11
St.-Apern-Strasse　22, 23
Stadtmauer (City Wall)　10, 60, 85, 86, 94 f.
Stollwerck-Passage　88, 104
Stollwerckgelände　90
Südstadt (South Side)　25, 89 ff.

Taubenbrunnen (Pigeon Fountain)　61

Ulrepforte (Gate)　85, 94
University　11, 13

Wallraf-Richartz-Museum　14, 16, 29, 39 ff.
WDR　88, 101 f.

140

Photo Credits:

Bayer AG, Leverkusen: p. 19

Fridmar Damm, Cologne: p. 53, 72, 102

Ford-Werke (factory), Cologne: p. 18

Rainer Gaertner, Bergisch Gladbach: Front flap, inside title page (p. 2/3), p. 7/8, 17, 21, 34, 36, 37, 39, 40/41, 43, 45, 46/47, 49, 50/51, 55, 56, 58, 60, 62, 65, 67, 70/71, 73, 74, 76, 79, 81, 82, 89, 93, 95 (top), 97, 103, 112, back flap

Friedrich Gier, Bonn: p. 108

Peter Ginter, Lohmar: Front jacket photo, p. 32, 33, 52, 56, 77, 89, 90, 101, 104/105, 110, 111, 118, 122, 124, 125, 126, 131

Kölner Verkehrsbetriebe AG, Cologne: p. 136/137

Celia Körber-Leupold, Cologne: p. 68, 69, 75, 95 (bottom)

Kreissparkasse (City Savings Bank) of Cologne: p. 117

Rhenish Picture Archives, Cologne: p. 10/11, 12, 99

August Sander/Rhenish Picture Archives, Cologne: p. 15

Horst Schmidt-Brümmer, Cologne: p. 48

Hugo Schmölz, Cologne: p. 98

Karl-Hugo Schmölz, Cologne: p. 16

VISTA POINT TOUR: COLOGNE

For its readers, the Vista Point Verlag offers a 3-day city tour package based on the Cologne City Guide in cooperation with a well-known travel agency.

Request complete information and hotel details at no charge and no obligation from the Vista Point Verlag:

Package: 3 Days Cologne Exclusive Tour

- 2 days 4-star hotel accommodations
- 2 breakfast buffets
- 2 lunches in the Hotel
- 1 lunch in a typical Cologne brewery restaurant
- 1 dinner in the Colonius television tower »Restaurant Wintergarten«
- City tour of Cologne
- Guided tour of the Roman-Germanic Museum and the Cologne Cathedral

Price: DM 475,– per person in double room. Supplement for single room upon request. The offer is available depending on hotel space.

VISTA POINT VERLAG
Engelbertstr. 38 A · P.O. Box 27 05 72 · 5000 Cologne 1
Telephone: (02 21) 21 05 87/88 · Telefax: 02 21 23 41 91

CITY GUIDES FROM VISTA POINT:

Barbara Wimmer
3 x Munich – City Guide

132 pages with 70 color illustrations and 6 maps. Sitze: 21 x 10,5 cm. ISBN 3-88973-106-6.
In English and German.

Hannah Glaser-Blauth
3 x Frankfurt – City Guide

144 pages with 74 color illustrations and 5 maps. Size: 21 x 10,5 cm. ISBN 3-88973-098-1.
In English and German.

PICTURE BOOKS
Cologne

Photographed by Peter Ginter and Rainer Gaertner and with essays by Bernd Polster and Paul v. Naredi-Rainer.
144 pages with 134 color and 40 black-white illustrations. Size: 31,5 x 25,5 cm., linen. ISBN 3-88973-064-7. In English, German, French and Spanish.

Two outstanding photographers have attemptod to capture the characteristic face of the Rhine metropolis in new and extraordinary pictures. Cologne as an urban living space and important economic center; as a place of history and intersection of modern traffic routes; as the city of churches and the arts.

The Cologne Cathedral

by Arnold Wolff. 112 pages with 94 color and 33 black-white illustrations. Size: 31,5 x 25,5 cm, laminated softcover. ISBN 3-88973-105-8. In English and German.

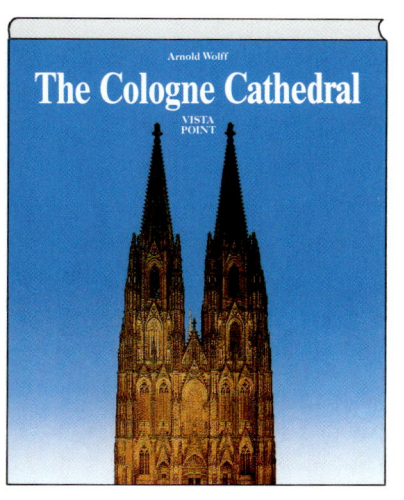

The picture book is authored by Arnold Wolff, present architect of the Cologne Cathedral, with photos by Rainer Gaertner, introduces readers to the long history of the building of the world-famous cathedral from the choir construction and the south tower, the building development during the Middle Ages, the period of stagnation and of decline and to the completion of the cathedral. The book recounts war destruction, damage by the elements, environmental problems and other recent events that the cathedral architect and his team have dealt with. In addition, the book describes the exemplary collection of cathedral art which dates from the Middle Ages and sketches the paraphernalia belonging to the cathedral dating from the Reformation to the present.

Front jacket photo: Severin bridge with Cologne Cathedral. Photo: Peter Ginter, Lohmar
Front flap: Cologne Cathedral. Photo: Rainer Gaertner, Bergisch Gladbach
Front inside flap: Cologne city plan.
Inside title page (p. 2/3): View from the west to the cathedral, in foreground, St. Gereon, on the right, Gross St. Martin, in background on the right, the Lufthansa building. Photo: Rainer Gaertner, Bergisch Gladbach
Back flap: View of the Cologne Cathedral. Photo: Rainer Gaertner, Bergisch Gladbach

Deutsche Bibliothek Cataloguing-in-Publication Data

[Three times Cologne]
3 × (days) Cologne : city guide / Horst Schmidt-Brümmer ; Paul v. Naredi-Rainer. Ill. Rainer Gaertner ... [Übers. aus d. Dt.: J. M. R. Arthur ; Kathleen Schaefer]. – Köln : Vista-Point-Verl., 1990
   Dt. Ausg. u. d. T. : Dreimal Köln
   ISBN 3-88973-097-3
NE: Schmidt-Brümmer, Horst [Mitverf.]; Gaertner, Rainer [Ill.]; Cologne

© 1990 Vista Point Verlag, Cologne
   All rights reserved
   Reproduction by Repro-Rózsa, Cologne
   Maps by Kartographie Huber, Munich
   Typeset, printed and bound by Rasch, Bramsche
   Translated by J. M. R. Arthur, Carson City, Nevada, and Kathleen Schaefer, Bad Soden
   Printed in West Germany
   ISBN 3-88973-097-3